The Lamonts of Lyndale

Harold S. MacLeod

with

A Biographical Sketch of the late Rev. Donald McDonald

Ewen Lamont, Elder

Selkirk
STORIES

ISBN 978-1-926494-36-4

The Lamonts of Lyndale © 2003 by Harold S. MacLeod
Republished with permission of the Estate of Harold S. MacLeod

A Biographical Sketch of the Late Rev. Donald McDonald is in the public domain.

Black-and-white sketches by Tilly MacLeod.

To record a family history is not the work of one person, it requires the input of many people. Unfortunately, space does not permit me to name everyone who contributed in so many ways, but special mention must be given to Betty Ludwick, Lillian Ross, Bonnie Swingle, Jean Pycock, Angus Lamont, Betty Tweedie, Myrtle Ballem, Hazel Frizzel, Laurie Gillingham, Wendy Graham, Carol Gillis, Dr. Roy Campbell, Marjorie Honeybourne, Elspeth Cleland, Richard and Winnie Hume, John Lamont, Glenda Gillis Graeme Martin, Eleanor MacDonald, Philip and Betty Compton, the late Bob Davidson, Marion Robbins, Don Frizzell, Keith Blair MacDonald, Helen Docherty, Angus Lamont, Maude Dodson, Kathleen Hudson, Donna Collings, Mae Stewart, Margaret Campion, as well as many others.

Special thanks are due also to the staff of the Provincial Archives, the Confederation Library and other provincial offices for their courtesy and cheerfulness in assisting in records research.

Special thanks as well to my wife Tilly for her assistance and patience in gathering all the pieces of information and assembling into a book form.

Harold S. MacLeod, 2002

Table of Contents

Introduction	7
Adieu, my Bonny Lyndale	9
Our Skye Roots	13
Lamonts in Skye	13
Early 18th Century Lamonts in Trotternish	13
Uig as the Probable Original Settlement Area	14
Peinchonnich and the Lamonts	15
Conneach Mac Uilliwimmvic Sheumais	16
Kenneth Williamson, Student of Law	16
William Lowman and Gullialmus Archijudex	19
Kenneth Williamson and Peinchonnich	20
Kenneth Williamson: Kenneth Lamont	21
Kenneth Williamson and the Lamonts of Lyndale	21
Lamonts of Skye and Lamonts of Cowal	23
The Lyndale Lamonts and their Pedigree	26
In Prince Edward Island	26
Forebears in Skye	27
The Lamonts of Lyndale	28
Malcolm Lamont and Elizabeth MacDonald	28
Ronald Lamont	31
John Lamont	44
Ewen Lamont	47
Malcolm Lamont	89
John Lamont	100
Angus Lamont	100
Sarah Lamont	104
Rebecca Lamont	110
Mary Elizabeth Lamont	130
Catherine Lamont	139
Rev. Murdoch Lamont	145

Rev. Donald MacDonald Lamont	158
Margaret Anne Lamont	161
Murdoch Lamont, Nephew of Malcolm the Pioneer	161
REV. DONALD MACDONALD	164
A Biographical Sketch of Rev. Donald McDonald	172
His Personal Appearance and Preaching	183
His First Pastoral Visit to Murray Harbour	188
Appendix to the Foregoing Sketch	195
INDEX	206

Harold S. MacLeod

Introduction

Harold MacLeod (1927-2014) was proud of his family. He was a descendant of both MacLeods and Lamonts (through his mother, Margaret MacNeill), while his wife was a Compton. He was proud of his ancestors, and of their persistence and fortitude in making better lives for themselves and their families in a new land, far from their ancestral Skye. He was proud of his contemporaries and their offspring for their learning and accomplishments. He never misses an opportunity to praise the achievements of members of the Lamont family, be they doctors, lawyers, pastors, authors, artists or performers. His own life is an example of the results of persistence and hard work. From early work on the railroad and in carpentry, he went on to become administrator of Riverview Manor and to serve as mayor of Montague.

This pride in his family may be part of Harold's motivation in investigating the genealogy of his family with dogged persistence. He published significant books: *The MacLeods of Prince Edward Island*; *The Loyalist Comptons*; *The Descendants of Roderick, Angus and Catherine MacNeill*; and this volume. The genealogical tables may be of interest mostly to descendants of the original Lamont settlers, but the narrative sections are of interest to anyone interested in the history, and especially the religious history, of Prince Edward Island.

The ministry of the charismatic Rev. Donald MacDonald affected all the founding members of the Lamont family of Prince Edward Island, beginning with Malcolm Lamont and Elizabeth MacDonald who moved to be closer to the Rev. MacDonald (p. 28). His influence may be found almost everywhere in this book, whether it be Rebecca Lamont in 1868, who, at the age of twelve, "danced in front of the elders' rail with all her might and main, like King David" in her joy at being set free from sin (p. 110), or Norman MacDonald, a soldier serving in the First World War, who upon hearing a "MacDonaldite hymn" from another tent, thought to himself, "These are my people, I am going up to see who they are" (p. 138). This is probably why Harold MacLeod, himself an elder in the Free Church of Scotland, concluded his book with a section about the Rev. Mr. MacDonald, although Mr. MacDonald was not a Lamont descendant.

As publisher of this book, I am grateful to the executor of Harold MacLeod's will, Margaret Campion, for granting permission to republish the book in a new edition. I am even more grateful to her for giving me several boxes of Harold's papers, including many of the papers used in preparing this book. Among those papers was a complete copy of Ewen Lamont's book, *A Biographical Sketch of the late Rev. Donald McDonald*. It seemed fitting to include this book as part of this new edition of Harold MacLeod's book.

Thanks are also due to A. Michael Shumate for his patient answers to my many questions about InDesign software and his generous tutorial in the use of PhotoShop.

While the genealogical tables in this edition remain unchanged from the original edition, this edition of *The Lamonts of Lyndale* includes several changes. Only photographs of earlier generations, the Lamonts of the 19th and early 20th century, have been included. The selection of poems by Lamont descendants at the end of the book has been replaced by Ewen Lamont's account of the life and influence of the Rev. Donald MacDonald. A complete index of all the names in the book is provided. Finally, the book was edited to ensure consistency of spelling and punctuation and to eliminate some redundancies.

John Westlie
Publisher, Selkirk Stories
Meadowbank, Prince Edward Island

Adieu, my Bonny Lyndale

My dear old home is now no more,
They've gone and left thee, Lyndale,
But while I live a sigh I'll give
For my happy home in Lyndale.

The sun was born behind thy hills
The moon belongs to Lyndale,
And the bright stars tell silent tales
Of how they came from Lyndale.

'Twas God that made them all, I know,
'Twas God that made thee, Lyndale,
For this they told me when a babe
As I fondly gazed on Lyndale.

How oft my bare feet measured all
The soft green fields of Lyndale,
The hills, the glens, the little streams
And the woody paths of Lyndale.

The meeting house, the school, the farm,
Held many a charm in Lyndale,
The foe was rare, the friend was warm,
In the sunny land of Lyndale.

We'll gather round the hearth no more
Dear sisters and dear brothers,
To hear the sayings wise and true
Of father and of mother.

To youthful dreams I wave adieu
They'll ne'er come true, oh Lyndale,
For real life began to dawn
On the morn I left thee, Lyndale.

Adieu, adieu, forevermore
They've gone and left thee, Lyndale,
But until I die I'll give a sigh
For the bygone days of Lyndale,

Composed in 1896 by Catherine Lamont

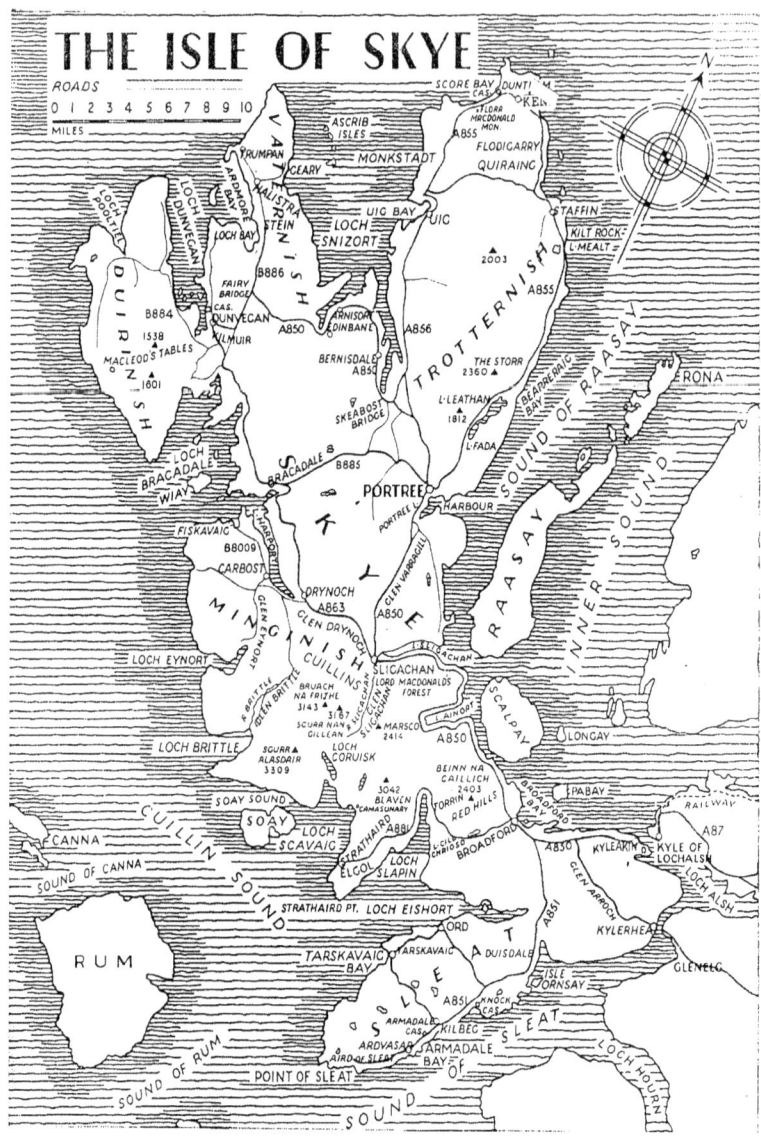

Our Skye Roots
by
William Dawson Lamont

In 1977, when in Scotland, we made the first of several visits with William Dawson Lamont and his wife, who was Ann Christie. I asked him if he had any information on the background of our family of Lamonts. He had notes which he said he would gather into a cohesive form and send to me. In the following paper he attempts to show the Lamonts of Lyndale lineage back to the 1400s. H.S.M.

Lamonts in Skye

Early 18th Century Lamonts in Trotternish

In an attempt to discover something of the origins of the Skye Lamonts, enquiries were made in the Island in the early 1930s. One suggestion locally offered was that they had been driven from Cowel by the persecution of the Campbells, the reference being pretty obviously to the Civil War of the 1640s. It is, of course, possible that some Lamonts did settle in Skye at this time or later, but there is no evidence that the activities of MacCallien Mor and his henchmen were ever instrumental in driving Lamonts so far north. The suggestion is probably based on nothing more substantial than the good old maxim, 'When in doubt, blame the Campbells.'

What the evidence does indicate is that the Lamonts were established in the Island well before the middle of the 17th century. Their distribution in Trotternish in the early part of the 18th is such as to suggest that the original settlement must have been at least a century–more probably two centuries–earlier.

Local records, unfortunately, are not very helpful, owing to a fire which, in the late 1920s, destroyed many of the older papers in the Estate Offices in Portree, the earliest Trotternish records there now going back only to the early 18th century. The most important paper is a Rental (apparently incomplete) for 1733. There is an earlier Rental (also apparently incomplete) for 1718–22 amongst the Forfeited Estates papers in the Register House, Edinburgh.

The broad conclusions to be drawn from the material are these: Lamonts were established in Trotternish, and apparently in no other part of Skye, in the early years of the century.

Uig (Westside) as the Probable Original Settlement Area

The actual distribution of Lamonts in the 18th and 19th century Trotternish: down to the year 1734 they are all concentrated, with three exceptions, in the northern part of the peninsula, north of a line from the River Conon (flowing into Uig Bay on the west) to the River Brogaig (flowing into Staffin Bay on the east). The three exceptions are: Donald and Malcolm Lamont in Renitra (near the present Snizort Church) in 1718-22; Malcolm Lamond in Peanichuillean (apparently included in the present Borve midway between Snizort Church and Portree) in 1733; and John Lamond in Valtos in 1733. Apart from these there are no references to Lamonts south of the Conon-Brogaig line until 1777 when we find a family at Maligar in Strathmartin.

North of the Conon-Brogaig line the distribution down to 1733 is as follows: On the Westside, the main concentration is round Uig Bay in the lower reaches of Glen Conon and Glen Rha, but Lamonts are also sprinkled towards the north as far as Erisco above Duntulm.

On the Eastside, there is one group in the Digg district just north of the River Brogaig, but with the exception of John in Valtos, there has been no spread, either north of south, from Digg to balance the spread from Uig on the Westside.

If one studies this distribution in relation to the topography of Trotternish (an inch or half-inch contour map is a useful guide), the most natural inference is that the main settlement has been north of the Conon round Uig Bay; and that from this main settlement there has been a spread up the Westside and a migration through the 'Bealach' to Staffin Bay on the Eastside; but had it been so, it is most unlikely that there would have been no substantial spread either north or south from Digg until long after a migration through Bealach to Uig had founded a considerable colony there and then fanned out over the north to above Duntulm.

Two conclusions, then, can be drawn with reasonable confidence. In the first place, we may assume that the original settlement was on the Westside round Uig Bay. Secondly, the early 16th century distribution indicates that the Lamonts must have been in the northern part of Trotternish for a very considerable period before the date of the earliest surviving records.

Peinchonnich and the Lamonts

On the north side of the River Conon there is a small district or 'township' called Peinchonnich which means 'Kenneth's Pennyland'. Our first notice of it is in 1722 when it was occupied by 'Angus McOil Vaine' (Angus son of Donald Bane) whom we know to be a Lamont, the great-great-grandfather of Miss Lamont, postmistress in Uig at the time of our visit in 1931. The holding was occupied by Lamonts until well on in the 19th century, and the local tradition is that 'there were always Lamonts in Peinchonnich.' The Kenneth after whom the lands are called is a shadowy figure.

An old man living in Glen Conon, whom we were recommended to consult as versed in old tradition, could say little more than that 'Kenneth was a great chief of long ago who lived there.' He was not (in the opinion of our informant) a MacDonald or a MacLeod but 'a stranger from some other family or clan.' The old man added, 'there were six good crofts in the township, and Kenneth owned them all as well as the big hill behind!'

To summarize our results so far: Down to the latter part of the 18th century the Lamonts in Skye seem to have been concentrated in Trotternish: the main–though not necessarily the original–settlement was on the Westside, round Uig Bay, down to the mid-18th century: in this area of the main concentration is a small district called Peinchonnich which, from time immemorial, had been inhabited by Lamonts. It was named after a personage of olden days who did not, according to local tradition, belong to any of the well known Skye clans: the Lamonts of Lyndale, P.E.I., trace to a Kenneth who was a man of some standing in his day. It is therefore possible–with a certain degree of probability–that the ancestor of the Lyndale Lamonts is the Kenneth of Peinchonnich.

Conneach Mac Uilliwimmvic Sheumais

Kenneth Williamson, Student of Law, 1508

It is also probable that he is the Kenneth who appears in the State Papers of James IV. The following occurs in the Register of the Privy Seal under No. 1654:

> 11 April 1508.–A letter of gift maid to Kanoch Williamson enduring the Kingis will of all and hale his landis of Terunga of Kilmartin and the half of Terunga of Baronesmore in Trouternes, with their pertinentis, extending nearly to sax merkis of auld extent, liand in the lordship of the Ilys,–to hold the said Kanoch as the skolis and for to lere and study the kingis lawis of Scotland and efterwart to exers and use the sammyn within the bondis of the Ilis, etc.

It appears that, unlike so many transactions of the period, this was no mere book entry, for Nicholson in his *History of*

Skye refers to Kenneth's return, and in *Transactions of the Gaelic Society of Inverness*, vol. xxx, Mr. J.G. MacKay of Portree writes:

> Some years afterwards, when the said Coinneach Mac Uilleim, or Kenneth the son of William, was a full-fledged lawyer, we find him collecting the King's cess in Kilmuir. Donald Gorm had omitted for some years to pay his public burdens; and the Government took the same means with him which his descendants did with others many a time since: they arrested his rents. Coinneach was employed on the job.

In case this reference to 'collecting the king's cess' may seem an historical howler, it has to be remembered that Skye had been detached from the Earldom of Ross and included in the Lordship of the Isles, and when the Lordship was annexed by the Crown in 1493 all dues hitherto paid to the Lord now belonged to the Crown.

At the same time, it does seem implausible that the effective royal authority should be dependent on a man who otherwise possessed no great local standing. The provision for Kenneth's education was part of the king's plan to supersede the old law and custom of the Isles by Lowland institutions. For this purpose he would work through the local magnates whenever possible, and, failing these, through agents who were already in positions of consequence in their areas. Thus, in 1505, as we learn from the Exchequer Rolls, it was MacIan of Ardnamurchan, already bailie of Islay under the last MacDonald, Lord of the Isles, who was appointed to carry out the administrative reformation in that Island. In Skye the king's bailie should obviously have been someone who already carried sufficient weight with Donald Gorm of Sleat and Trotternish to make his work possible; and even under the most favourable conditions, if Donald was disinclined to pay his dues no administrative officer could have done much about it.

But though the idea of a successful arrest of Donald's rents is unconvincing, the important point is that Kenneth did in fact return to Skye (if any reliance can be placed on local tradition). One would therefore suspect that he was a close relative or cadet of the MacDonalds of Sleat. However, Dr. A. MacDonald of Kilearnan considered this to be unlikely. While he was, of course, familiar with the Privy Seal entry, he found nothing to suggest a MacDonald connection. An alternative possibility would seem to be that Kenneth was a MacLeod, since historically the MacLeods were as deeply involved in Trotternish as the MacDonalds. But Canon MacLeod was not in the least disposed to lay claim to the mysterious scholar, not even when we mentioned the family of MacLeods who went under the name of 'McWilliam.' Actually the 'McWilliam' sept of MacLeods in Skye was a pure coincidence as we found from the Gaelic version of Mr. MacKay's paper in the *Trans. Gael. Soc. Inverness.*

There, Kenneth's grandfather is also mentioned. He was 'Coinneach mac Uilleim mhic Sheumais'–Kenneth son of William son of James. The 'Williamson' or 'MacWilliam' is clearly not a surname. It simply indicates the Christian name of Kenneth's father.

Another interesting–and probably the most fruitful–suggestion is that Kenneth belonged to one of the hereditary administrative families in the Isles, such as the Morrisons, of the Long Island, Nicholsons of Trotternish and McBriuns of Islay. They seem to have combined the offices of custodian and consultant of the law and some form of 'magistracy.' It is thus possible that Kenneth's forebears were 'lawmen' in this sense. Of course the law they expounded or applied was the ancient Celtic law as it had evolved throughout Hebridean history; and it may be that Kenneth was chosen from such a family to lead the substitution of 'the king's laws of Scotland' for the Celtic law and customs of the west.

William Lowman, 1507, and Gullialmus Archijudex, 1485

With this possibility in mind we turn to another entry in the Register of the Privy Seal (No. 1522) under the date 1507, just the year prior to that in which Kenneth MacWilliam's grant is made:

> Ane protection made to Johne McGillemartyne, Mr. Martyne Makgillemartyne, Mulchoill, Huchone McGillemartyne and William Lowman , with the tennandis of our landis of Trotternish liand within the erldom of Ros and lordship of the Ilis

It is rather odd that Trotternish should be given both its older and later status as within the earldom of Ross and the Lordship of the Isles, but the main point of interest is that we find a William Lowman in the company of Rev. Martin Martin (rector of the parish at that time), two other Martins and Malcolm Nicholson. The Nicholsons at one time served as 'maors' for at least part of Trotternish. The Martins, under the older form of MacGillemartin, were probably descended from members of an ancient religious community in Kilmartin, and they were later used as administrative officers by the MacDonalds. William Lowman must have been included in the group in virtue of some office, and 'Lowman' naturally suggests 'lawman.' It is, in his case, pretty obviously a surname, and one may infer that it has come to stand both for the office and as a family name.

This suggestion that William was a man of law is encouraged by the existence of a charter (Register House Charters, no. 517) granted in 1485 by Angus, Master of the Isles and Lord of Trotternish, conveying certain lands in Mull to the Abbey of Iona. It was witnessed by (amongst others):

> Lacclanno McMurghaich archipoeta (the bard McVurish)

> Gullialmo archjudice (William, chief lawman)
> Colino Fergussii domini cancellario (chancellor: a Mac-Beath?)

The William of 1485 could well be the William of 1507– some twenty-two years later. And the suggestion that Kenneth Williamson belonged to a hereditary family of 'lawmen' would tend to be supported by the entry referring to William Lowman irrespective of the question whether William Lowman and Gullialmus archijudex are one and the same person.

Kenneth Williamson and Peinchonnich

Whatever may be in doubt, it is virtually certain that Kenneth Williamson of 1508 is the Kenneth from whom Peinchonnich derived its name. The lands given to support his education were the terunga of Kilmartin and half the terunga of Baronesmore. The terunga of Kilmartin is easily located. It consisted of lands on the Eastside in the vicinity of Kilmartin River. Baronesmore does not appear on current maps, but there is an old map which has 'Baronefs' just off the coast of Uig Bay. 'Bar an eas mhor' is the obvious reading–the 'bar' of the big waterfall. 'Bar' might stand for 'borg' (a strong point, or perhaps a village); or it might signify 'barr' (a height or hill). There is evidence in support of any one of these derivations. But whichever we take, Peinchonnich would fall within the terunga of Baronesmore, the 'eas mhor' being, without any doubt, the fall of the River Rha just before it enters into Uig Bay.

From all this, one inference seems fully justified. Our informant in Glen Conon had said that Peinchonnich was named after a 'great chief of long ago who lived there,' not a MacDonald or MacLeod but 'a stranger from some other family or clan,' and 'he owned the six good crofts in the township as well as the big hill behind.' This description of the lands 'owned' by Kenneth puts him in the social class which in succeeding ages was appropriate to one of the great 'tacksmen' in the sense that he had a 'township' and its common moorland which would be farmed by a number of tenants. The lands in question were certainly in the terunga of Baronesmore, half of which was given to Kenneth Williamson; and the only reasonable conclusion would seem to be that Kenneth Williamson and the Kenneth of Peinchonnich are one and the same person.

Kenneth Williamson: Kenneth Lamont

The cumulative force of the argument points to the conclusion that Kenneth Williamson was Kenneth Lamont. The conclusion is indeed that to which we are led whether we work from the basis of Kenneth Williamson's presumed ancestry or from what we know of Peinchonnich. (a) From the point of view of his ancestry, we may take it that Kenneth was selected for training in the reformed administration of the Isles, not as a member of one of the great landed families, but as a member of a family of hereditary lawyers. Laman (Lamond) or MacLaomuinn (Lamont) must have become by then the family surname as we find 'William Lowman' in the preceding year. (b) As to Peinchonnich, we know that it was occupied by Lamonts 'from time immemorial' and the presumption is that the Kenneth after whom the lands were called was their progenitor. The two lines of argument (a) and (b) reinforce each other when we observe that Peinchonnich is in fact within the terunga, half of which was given to Kenneth Williamson, thus pointing to Kenneth son of William as the progenitor of the Lamonts of Peinchonnich.

Kenneth Williamson and the Lamonts of Lyndale

The main purpose of this investigation is to support the view that Kenneth Williamson is almost certainly the progenitor of the Lamonts of Lyndale, P.E.I. That he was a Lamont is supported by evidence independent of the pedigree preserved by this family, and the only remaining question is whether he can be identified with the Kenneth with which that pedigree begins. The presumption is that we are dealing with the same person, a presumption which should stand unless positive arguments can be raised against it.

I think the only doubts which might be entertained concern the time factor: could the Kenneth of the pedigree have been a youth or young man in 1508?

We have seen that Murdoch Buie (No. 9 in the pedigree below) must have been born in 1725/30. There are six generations of Murdoch's forbears back to (and including) Kenneth; and if we count 25 years to the generation this will give the date of Kenneth's birth as 1575–over three-quarters of a century too late. But in the event of the pedigree having come down through younger sons the average for the generations must be much greater. This is in fact what has happened for the latest period covered by the pedigree. Thus we have William Dawson, 1901, Murdoch, 1865, Ewen, 1817–a period of 84 years between the births of grandfather and grandson. Again, the grandfather of Ewen was born not later than 1730–a further 87 years. This gives the average for the last four generations counting from Murdoch Buie as 42/3 years. At this rate Kenneth could have born in 1471. It is, of course, most unlikely that the average was so great over the whole period of the pedigree, but the succession of names does suggest that we are for the most part dealing with younger sons. In no case do we have a grandson bearing the name of his grandfather, as we should normally have if the grandson had been the eldest of the father.

We may say, therefore, that there is no reason on chronological grounds for rejecting the identification of Kenneth Williamson with Kenneth the ancestor of the Lamonts of Lyndale.

Lamonts of Skye and Lamonts of Cowal

The relation of the Lamonts of Skye to those of Cowal is not a principal issue in this paper, the problem being so complex that there is no particular hypothesis with a clear advantage over others. It could be that the Lamonts in the Hebrides–in Skye, Tiree, Mull–are of independent origin, descendants of the 'lawmen' of these islands. On the other hand there is no incompatibility between the foregoing argument and a direct connection with Cowal. The Cowal clan had surprisingly distant ramifications in the 15th and 16th centuries–in Perth, Fife, Angus, Aberdeen. Lamonts in France were descended from a James Lamont married to 'Jean of Perth' in 1460. She must have belonged to the family of Drummond which, according to tradition, had a considerable influence on the fortunes of the Lamont Chief's family at that time.

Perhaps the most interesting tradition in this connection is the one which asserts a link with Skye. Robert V of Lamont married Anne, daughter of Donald, 2nd Lord of the Isles, and one of his sons is said to have been the ancestor of the Bourdons of Feddal in Perthshire.

In 1699, replying to an enquiry from the son of the then laird of Feddal, Archibald XV explains how this came about. On an occasion when the court of King Robert III was in Bute, a number of his retainers crossed to Toward where they were slain in a quarrel with Lamont's sons. The young men then dispersed to escape the royal wrath, and (continues the laird) "your predecessor going to the countrie where you now live in a mean condition by occasion of the disasture of the families, having nothing in his hand but a foursquare staffe in old Highlands called Bourdouich with which he fought gallantlie Pearths for predecessor then laird of a place called Stopha, so your surname began as my father told me truly ..." (Lamont Papers, p. 314)

But more than half a century earlier, Henry V of Feddal had given a different account. According to him the first of the name of Bourdon lived in the Isle of Skye, and "efter king Edgar the 4th sone of Malcolm Canmoir beat Donald the usurper, who did fley to the Isle of Skey and was there taken and brought to Edgar who asking who did take him was answered Sholto ferr le burden dou for which he had considerable lands there given him, and retained the nam always, the familie long after falling to a daughter who was heiress she was married to one of Lamonts sons who took on his wifes name, he coming doun to Perthshire met with Drummon of Stobhall whom he assist in some quarrel … who did gift him som lands in Perthshire … and selling his highland interest did make a purchas there." (Lamont Papers, p. 315)

While both of these accounts are historically suspect in detail as well as being incompatible with each other, it is interesting that the one account makes the first Bourdon a son of Robert V of Lamont who married Anne of the Isles, while the other marries a laird of Lamont's son to a Skye heiress. Drummond of Stobhall figures in both accounts as a patron of young Lamont-Bourdon, and it may or may not be significant that Drummond was Justiciary for Scotland at the time when, according to the Laird of Lamont's account, the slaughter of the king's couriers took place at Toward.

However, these unsystematic comments on the possibility of a Cowal connection are merely appended as a footnote, not as part of the main argument.

This paper shows that, while strict proof is lacking, the present writer, William Dawson Lamont, is almost certainly descended in the male line from the Kenneth Williamson who figures in the State Papers of 1508, and that the said Kenneth is most probably the son of the William 'Archijudex' who witnessed a charter of Angus, Master of the Isles and Lord of Trotternish, in 1485. The pedigree thus claimed is as follows:

(1) James

(2) William ('archijudex,' 1485; 'Lowman,' 1507)

(3) Kenneth ('Williamson,' 1508; of 'Peinchonnich,' traditional ancestor of 'Lamonts of Lyndale, P.E.I.')

(4) Duncan

(5) Murdoch

(6) Donald

(7) Duncan

(8) John (living at Valtos, Eastside, Trotternish, Skye, 1733)

(9) Murdoch 'Buie' (fought in '45 and therefore born not later than 1730)

(10) Malcolm m. Ishbel (or Elizabeth) MacDonald (emigrated to P.E.I., Canada, 1829)

(11) Ewen (6th son) born in Bernisdale, in the Lyndale district of Skye in 1817, m. Sarah MacPherson.

(12) Murdoch (4th son, b. 1865) m. Euphemia Ann Hume.

(13) William Dawson Lamont (4th son, b. 1901) m. Ann Fraser Christie.

In elucidating the claim it will be best to leave aside for the moment the first two persons named–James and William–

and start with the remainder of the pedigree from Kenneth (No. 3) down. This is a traditional genealogy preserved by the writer's family in Prince Edward Island, known as the Lyndale Lamonts. Some references in notes by my late father, Rev. Murdoch Lamont (No. 12) who died as minister of Rothiemurchus in 1927, dealing with our forbears in Skye, induced me to ask my uncle, Rev. Donald Lamont, then resident in Canada, for fuller information. He sent me this English version of the pedigree which had been given to him in Gaelic by his father Ewen (No. 11). He was "Donald, son of Ewen, son of Malcolm, son of Murdoch Buie, son of John, son of Duncan, son of Donald, son of Murdoch, son of Duncan, son of Kenneth." My uncle was satisfied that the version he sent me was the one he had received, for as a boy he had once made an error in repeating it to an old relative who was scandalized, making him repeat and repeat the correct version to fix it in his mind.

The Lyndale Lamonts and their Pedigree

In Prince Edward Island

Although my father Murdoch (12) and his younger brother Donald were both educated in the University of Glasgow and became ministers of the Church of Scotland. They were born in Lyndale, P.E.I., my father in 1865. Their father Ewen (11) was born in 1817 in Bernisdale, which is in the Lyndale district of Skye, and he was brought to P.E.I. as a boy when his father, Malcolm, emigrated there in 1829. At the time of their arrival, the upper reaches of the Orwell River had no distinctive name, and it was on Ewen's proposal that it was later given the name 'Lyndale' which it bears today. Ewen, less interested in his farm than his books, was for some time the local schoolmaster and unofficial consultant in all public affairs, and he is described by Malcolm MacQueen in *Skye Pioneers and the Island* as "a worthy member of a talented family." He married

Sarah, daughter of John MacPherson (from Badenoch it is understood) and Mary Currie; and they had 5 sons and 8 daughters. Ewen's father Malcolm (10) was born on the East-side of Trotternish, Skye, presumably at Valtos. He married Ishbel (or Elizabeth) daughter of Angus MacDonald. Of their 7 sons (there is no mention of daughters), 5 were born on the East Side: but about 1816 Malcolm moved to Bernisdale, where Ewen and his younger brother were born. Malcolm was a fairly prosperous cattle drover who kept a bank account in Inverness; and on emigrating to Canada in 1829 he took all the family with the exception of his eldest son who died as a soldier in India.

Forebears in Skye

Malcolm's father Murdoch Buie (9) lived in Eastside, Trotternish, and is said to have built boats and violins. He must have been an interesting character as he joined the unofficial contingent which followed Prince Charles in the '45. This would place his birth at perhaps 1725–surely not later than 1730. The name of his wife is unknown and we have no information of children other than Malcolm.

Murdoch's father John (8) was living at Valtos in 1733. Beyond this we know nothing of him; and of his ancestors we have merely the names–Duncan, Donald, Murdoch, Duncan–until we come to Kenneth (3). Though Kenneth himself is little more than a name to us, the name at one time seems to have been one to conjure with, the genealogical fragment stopping with him for the apparently all sufficient reason that 'he was a great man in his day.'

The Lamonts of Lyndale

Malcolm Lamont and Elizabeth MacDonald

Now begins the list of the descendants of Malcolm Lamont and his wife Elizabeth MacDonald, who was a daughter of Angus MacDonald of Skye. She had a sister Frances who accompanied them to P.E.I. and later married Ewen Ross, son of John Ross of Flat River, P.E.I., who came over from Skye on the *Polly* in 1803. They also had with them Malcolm's nephew, Murdock Lamont, who later settled in Springton, and married Catherine Stewart. Malcolm and Elizabeth emigrated from the Isle of Skye in 1829 on the *Mary Kennedy* and settled for a short time in Vernon River or Millview. They moved from there to Orwell Rear or Back Settlement, later named Lyndale, to be near the Rev. Donald MacDonald and his headquarters at Orwell Head. Malcolm MacQueen in his book *Skye Pioneers and the Island*, referring to the *Mary Kennedy* settlers, states that:

> *Argosy* never sailed with more precious cargo than that discharged at Charlottetown on June the 1st, 1829, from the good ship *Mary Kennedy*. There were 84 heads of families in the party. They settled along the Murray Harbour road, and in the Back Settlement, later called Lyndale. Each family bought from fifty to one hundred acres of land … Perhaps in the history of the migration of the human race no more high minded and worthy people ever entered a new land than those who came out on the *Mary Kennedy*. Their heritage of piety persisted for several generations in their new home.

Also in *Skye Pioneers*, he includes an item from the *P.E.I. Register and Gazette*, for June 2nd, 1829, stating:

> 84 Immigrants including women and children from the Isle of Skye arrived here on Sunday. They left their native

place about 6 weeks ago in a ship for Cape Breton along with a number of settlers for that Island. They seem all to be in high health and judging from appearances in easy circumstances.

With prudent foresight characteristic of their race they came provided with 12 months provisions and an ample stock of warm clothing.

They all have relatives already settled on the Island chiefly about Belfast, and with the exception of one family it is, we understand, their intention also to locate in that thriving settlement.

Malcolm and his wife Elizabeth, had a family of six sons, the eldest of which did not accompany his parents to Prince Edward Island. However Malcolm's brother's son named Murdock, came with them and settled in Springton, P.E.I.

Malcolm and Elizabeth's children were:

A1. Angus Lamont was born in Skye, did not come to Prince Edward Island. He was a soldier and was said to have fought in the American Civil War, he died unmarried on service in India.
A2. Murdoch Lamont was born in Skye, went to the U.S.A. and died unmarried.
A3. Donald Lamont, born in Skye, died in Halifax, Nova Scotia.

The following three sons settled on Prince Edward Island:

A4. William Lamont, son of Malcolm Lamont and Elizabeth MacDonald, born in Skye, was a schoolteacher and lived in Victoria Cross, P.E.I. He was the only one of this family of Lamonts to join the Free Church of Scotland.

Malcolm MacQueen, author of *Skye Pioneers and the Island*, recounting the founding of Valleyfield Church, states that:

William was an expert 'liner.' This was an important part of the precentor's duty, and it was well performed by him. At a time when each person in the audience did not possess a book, it was necessary, if all were to sing, for someone at the beginning of each line or two to intone the words in a voice heard by the whole audience. This was known as 'lining.' Once done each person had the words and was thereby enabled to raise his voice in song. All sang and sang fervently, and if all did not pray, those who did appropriated the time that would have been taken up by others if all had prayed. The result was hearty, refreshing singing, and long tedious prayers.

On one occasion

William Lamont was lining and all present were entering with the greatest fervour into the song. It was fall, and Boreas smote the humble cottage with bitter blasts. The household dog had been driven from his accustomed haunt beside the open hearth, to make way for the press of visitors. Towards the end of the first song, a dismal howling was set up by the faithful Achates without, his spirit moved as much by the mournful and unusual harmony within, as by the bitter blasts without.

At length the song was ended. The last note had scarcely died away before the precentor, in the same wavering tone, and with the same fervid expression, carried on in Gaelic, 'Chaidh Satan a steach do'n choin' (Satan has entered the dog). Thinking him still 'lining,' the congregation, swept along by the enthusiasm of the occasion, took up the refrain, and from every throat there arose, loud in unison, 'Chaidh Satan a steach do'n choin.'

William Lamont had a peculiar habit when he would visit a home, of not going directly to the entrance door, he would instead, walk around the house in a wide circle and would enter, only if invited by one of the residents within.

He never married.

Ronald Lamont

A5. Ronald Lamont, 1809-1896, son of Malcolm Lamont and Elizabeth MacDonald, was born in the Isle of Skye, emigrated to Prince Edward Island with his parents in 1829, m. Mary Ross, 1818-1884, daughter of Donald Ross and Christina MacDonald from Flat River. They lived at Victoria Cross, with issue:

    B1. Elizabeth Lamont, m. Malcolm MacKinnon, of Uigg, son of Duncan MacKinnon and Catherine MacLeod. They moved to Sydney N.S., and had issue:

        C1. Cyrus MacKinnon in Boston unmarried.

        C2. Mary MacKinnon died unmarried.

        C3. Catherine MacKinnon in Sydney N.S., unmarried.

        C4. Daniel MacKinnon of N.Y.

        C5. Sarah MacKinnon lived in Sask.

        C6. Flora MacKinnon married Mr. McLaughlin of Boston.

        C7. Ronald MacKinnon drowned in Sydney N.S., 1912, age 22.

        C8. Ewen MacKinnon

        C9. Lachlan MacKinnon unmarried.

        C10. Catherine MacKinnon, a teacher.

        C11. Sarah MacKinnon m. Lachlan MacDonald of Quincy, Mass., no issue.

    B2. Angus Lamont, 1851-1947, m. Christy MacLeod, 1855-1948, daughter of Donald MacLeod and Mary MacDonald, Victoria Cross. Angus and Christy farmed at Victoria Cross and had issue:

        C1. Silas Lamont, construction supervisor. He never married and was a veteran of WWI. He died in Edmonton, Alberta.

C2. James Lamont, owner of Pool Construction Co., Regina, Saskatchewan. He married late in life and had no family.
C3. Lizzie Lamont, 1883-1907, buried in Orwell Head.
C4. John Lamont, 1887-1896, buried in Orwell Head.
C4. Mary Lamont, 1890-1976. She worked for a bank in Charlottetown, never married.
C5. William Lamont, 1890-1952, twin of Mary. He farmed on the old home in Victoria Cross, never married.

B3. Murdock Lamont, 1853–1879, died June 19th, 1879, buried in Orwell Head.

B4. Christy Mary Lamont, 1855-1937, m. Roderick MacDonald, 1842-1916, Green Marsh, later named Bellevue. After Roderick's death, Christy and her youngest son Daniel sold the farm in Bellevue. She moved to Alberta to live with her daughter, and Daniel moved to Charlottetown where he was known as "Taxi Dan." Christina and Roderick are buried in Valleyfield. Their children were:

C1. Mary MacDonald, taught school on Prince Edward Island and later taught in Alberta where she married William Fallow who was at one time Minister of Highways for the province of Alberta. They lived in Vermillion, Alberta, with issue at least:

D1. Alexander Fallow, married in British Columbia, with issue:

E1. Adrian Fallow, m. Shelly Brown, living in B.C.
E2. Rod Fallow.
E3. Tracy Fallow.
E4. Lynn Fallow.

D2. Vanessa Fallow, m. Ian Chessor, living in Edmonton, with issue:

E1. David Chessor.

C2. John Ronald MacDonald, married in St. Albert,

Alberta, with a large family. He was at one time Deputy Warden at Fort Saskatchewan.

C3. Alexander MacDonald, m. Ada _____, from Sydney Mines, Cape Breton. They lived in Bon Accord, Alberta, where he had a car dealership. Their children were:

    D1. Ronald MacDonald, killed in a car accident aged 20.

    D2. William MacDonald, married and living in Whitehorse, Yukon, with issue:

        E1. Joseph MacDonald, Professor of Architecture at Harvard University.

        E2. Stuart MacDonald, working on cruise ships.

        E3. Roderick MacDonald, married in Edmonton with a family.

C4. Katie Ann MacDonald, died July 26th, 1891, aged one year and one month.

C5. Daniel MacDonald (Donald), "Taxi Dan," 1891-1980, m. Edith Lillian Robbins, 1907-1980, daughter of Percy Robbins and Catherine Ladner, from Midgell, P.E.I. They had issue:

    D1. Sterling Leigh MacDonald, last thought to be living in Culver City, California, married with at least one son.

    D2. Donald Elmer MacDonald, m. Elizabeth Stokes, from Newfoundland. He lives in Hamilton, his children are:

        E1. Donald Richard MacDonald, serving in the Navy.

        E2. Chelsea MacDonald, living in Hamilton, Ontario.

        E3. Bobby MacKay, whose mother was Gloria MacKay.

    D3. Keith Blair MacDonald, m. Sandra Chetek. They live in Charlottetown, where he was a school

teacher. They had issue:
    E1. Keith Michael MacDonald, m. Lois Fanning, with issue:
        F1. Adam MacDonald.
        F2. Dustin MacDonald.
        F3. Carter MacDonald.
        F4. Mallory MacDonald.
    E2. Jennifer MacDonald, Ph.D. in Psychology, living in Edmonton.
    E3. Joanne MacDonald, lived one day. Two other children died prematurely.

B5. Sarah Lamont, b. 1858, died unmarried.

B6. Donald Lamont, m. 1) Margaret MacEachern, she died at age 34. They lived at Victoria Cross, with issue:
    C1. Ronald Lamont, baptized 1878, left the Island, never married.
    C2. Daniel Lamont, left the Island, never married.
    C3. Ewen Lamont, b. January 26th 1884, m. Ida____, lived in St. John, N.B., with issue:
        D1. Marjory Lamont, m. Roy Terry.
        D2. Jean Lamont, m. _____ Ferguson, living in California.
    C4. Mary Jannet Lamont, 1881-1971, m. Wellington N. Docherty, 1870–1929. They lived at Victoria Cross and had issue:
        D1. Florence Docherty, 1906–1992, m. Whitefield MacLeod, 1898–1979. They farmed in Grandview, and had issue:
            E1. Joan Margaret MacLeod, m. Gordon MacDougall, from Newtown, P.E.I. They live in Massachusetts, and had issue:
                F1. David MacDougall, m. Cynthia Ann Davis, with issue:
                    G1. Carrie Ann MacDougall, with issue:
                        H1. Courtney Nicole MacDougall.

      G2. Amy Christine MacDougall.
  F2. Nancy MacDougall, m. Richard Richmond, with issue:
      G1. Richard Boston Richmond.
  F3. Linda MacDougall and Steven Olson have issue:
      G1. Jessica Kristen Olson.
  F4. Phillip MacDougall, m. Sheri Lynn Karjouski, with issue:
      G1. Corey Steven MacDougall.
      G2. Ashley Joan MacDougall.
      G3. Philip Whitfield MacDougall.
  F5. Janet MacDougall, m. 1) Steven Volpe, with issue:
      G1. Anthony David Volpe.
      G2. Alicia Victoria Volpe.
  Janet m. 2) Antonio Cirone, with issue:
      G3. Joseph Frederico Cirone.
E2. John MacLeod, m. Mary Masters, living in Grandview, no family.
D2. Margaret Docherty, m. Dan Cummings, who was a merchant in Vernon, P.E.I. They had one son:
  E1. Donald Cummings, m. Irene Hussey, from Newfoundland. They live in Halifax, N.S., where he is a bank manager. They have two children:
    F1. David Cummings.
    F2. Tracy Cummings.
D3. Louise Docherty, m. Ivor Estifjord, living in Seattle, Oregon. They had one daughter:
  E1. Jane Estifjord, not married.
D4. Willard Docherty, 1912–1999, m. Helen Coyle. They lived in Montague, with issue:
  E1. Glen Docherty, m. Linda Beale, living in Montague, with issue:
    F1. Jeffery Docherty.

F2. Denise Docherty, m. Steven MacDonald, living in Charlottetown.

E2. Elaine Docherty, m. Butch Stewart, Montague, with issue:

F1. Martin Stewart, m. Teena Hicken. They live in Charlottetown, with issue:

G1. Jonathon Stewart.

F2. Wade Stewart, m. Jennifer Ward, from Fredericton. They live in Brooklyn, P.E.I., with issue:

G1. Emma Stewart.

G2. Halle Stewart.

F3. Bonnie Stewart, m. Donald Munro, living in Quebec, with issue:

G1. Amanda Munro.

G2. Alexander Munro.

F4. Scott Stewart, m. Rene Delladance, from Fredericton. They both teach in Charlottetown, with issue:

G1. Anna Stewart.

F5. Jayson Stewart.

Elaine Docherty m. 2) Dale Murphy, Charlottetown.

E3. Kenneth Docherty, m. Edith MacPherson, with two children:

F1. Shane Docherty, graduate engineer.

F2. Sonia Docherty, university graduate (criminology).

E4. Cyril Docherty, m. Edith Whiteway, living in Brooklyn, P.E.I., with issue:

F1. Jonathon Docherty.

F2. Erin Docherty, attending university (journalism).

F3. Alexander Docherty, attending university.

F4. Matthew Docherty, attending university.
C5. Sarah Isabella Lamont, b. February 15th 1886, daughter of Donald Lamont and Margaret MacEachern, m. Sydney MacIntyre, Montague, with issue:
- D1. Edith MacIntyre, m. Rollie MacIntyre, living in Long Beach, California.
- D2. Reta MacIntyre, m. James Burns, living in Long Beach, California, with issue:
  - E1. Debbie Burns.
- D3. Claude MacIntyre, married in Massachusetts with two daughters.

C6. Gillane Lamont, b. August 18, 1887, married late in life and had no family. He died in British Columbia.

Donald Lamont married 2) Margaret MacPhee, daughter of Malcolm MacPhee and Flora MacLeod, Heatherdale. They had issue:

C7. Malcolm Lamont, 1890–1924, m. Gladys VanIderstine, daughter of Peter VanIderstine and Eleanor Bears. They lived in Victoria Cross with issue:
- D1. Peggy Lamont, 1920–2001, m. Douglas Nicholson, who was killed in the Korean War, in 1954, age 34, leaving two sons:
  - E1. James Nicholson, m. Beverly Oatway. They live in St. John and have two children:
    - F1. Geordie Nicholson.
    - F2. Sarah Nicholson.
  - E2. Randolph Nicholson, single, living in St. John, N.B.
- D2. Ruth Lamont, m. George Bowley, 1919–2002, Midgell, with issue:
  - E1. Preston Bowley, m. Diane MacDougall. They live in Charlottetown, with a daughter:
    - F1. Deanna Bowley.
  - E2. Wayne Bowley, m. Cathy Jackson, Midgell,

with issue:
    F1. James Bowley.
    F2. Gregory Bowley.
    F3. Richard Bowley.
    F4. Stephen Bowley.
E3. Anna Bowley, m. Garfield Anderson, Charlottetown, with issue:
    F1. Erin Anderson, m. Chad Griffin.
    F2. Glen Anderson.
    F3. Kurt Anderson.
E4. Joan Bowley, single, living in Charlottetown.
E5. Eric Bowley, m. Donna _____, Midgell, with issue:
    F1. Colin Bowley.
    F2. Nicolle Bowley.
    F3. Ryan Bowley.

D3. Eleanor Lamont, m. Moody MacDonald, Roseneath, with issue:
    E1. Gladys MacDonald, m. Elwood MacIntyre, Montague, issue:
        F1. Michele MacIntyre, m. Alex Rogers, living in New Haven, P.E.I., with issue:
            G1. John Thomas Rogers.
            G2. Kristie Rogers.
    E2. Elizabeth MacDonald, killed in an auto accident in 1960, age 14 years.
    E3. Kenneth MacDonald, m. Glenda Graham, Roseneath, issue:
        F1. Steven MacDonald.
        F2. Craig MacDonald.
        F3. Andrew MacDonald.
    E4. Donald MacDonald, m. 1) Debbie White, living in Roseneath with issue:
        F1. Kari Lynn MacDonald.
        F2. Amanda Jean MacDonald.

Donald married 2) Della Campbell.
E5. Garry MacDonald, m. 1) Terry MacAree, with issue:
F1. Robert MacDonald.
Garry married 2) Carla Webster, with issue:
F2. Taylor MacDonald.
F3. Neil MacDonald.
F4. William Duff MacDonald.
D4. Donald Lamont, m. Margaret Rattray. They live in Roseneath, with issue:
E1. Debra Lamont, m. Darryl MacLean, New Perth, issue:
F1. Marshall MacLean.
F2. Morgan MacLean.
E2. Douglas Lamont, m. Nancy Webster, with issue:
F1. Matthew Lamont.
F2. Benjamin Lamont.
F3. Jonathon Lamont.
F4. Jacob Lamont.
E3. Donna Lamont, m. Terry Coates, with issue:
F1. Rebecca Coates.
F2. Coady Coates.
B7. Malcolm Lamont, 1849–1918, m. Catherine Cantelo, 1863–1919, daughter of John Cantelo and Mary MacKinnon. They lived in Montague, later moved to Sydney, Nova Scotia. Catherine died in Charlottetown and is buried in the People's Cemetery. A local paper carried the following notice on Malcolm's death:

Deceased: Lamont; At the Victoria General Hospital, Halifax, Tuesday 28th inst. Mal. Lamont, of Sydney, formerly of Montague, P.E.I., aged 69 years. The remains were taken to his brother-in-law's Mal. MacKinnon, Furnace Street, Whitney Pier, burial in Eastmount Cemetery.

Malcolm and Catherine had issue:
   C1. Mary Lamont, b. 1883, earned her medical degree about 1912, in Boston, where she met and married her husband, Norman L. Bowen, from Kingston, Ontario. They lived in Chicago, where he was a geological physicist, and was the discoverer of the Bowen Reaction Series. This series accounts for the production of certain rocks. It is cited in encyclopedias and other reference books.
   They had issue:
      D1. Catherine Bowen, m. Jerrold Orne, with issue:
         E1. Mary Orne.
         E2. Jonathan Orne.
         E3. Jean Orne.
   C2. John Salmon Lamont, 1885-1964, K.C., M.L.A., Winnipeg. His obituary in a Winnipeg newspaper states that:

Mr. Lamont was born in Montague, Prince Edward Island and had lived in Manitoba since 1903. He was a graduate of Prince of Wales College, Charlottetown, and a graduate in Arts from Manitoba College, where he received the Gold Medal in mathematics in 1910. He received the Masters of Arts Degree in Mathematics and Mathematical Physics from Princeton University in 1911. Mr. Lamont studied law under the late Chief Justice Adamson, and received the University Gold Medal in Law on graduation in 1914 and the Law Society Gold Medal the same year, and practiced law for a time with the Hon. E.J. MacMurray, and subsequently with the Hon. F.M. Bastin. At his death Mr. Lamont was senior partner in the firm of Lamont, Buriak and Zivot. He was appointed King's Council in 1937.

Mr. Lamont served in France and Belgium with the Royal Canadian Artillery during the First World War. He was Honorary Life Member of the Liberal Party of Manitoba. He occupied a number of executive positions and was Member of The Legislative Assembly for Iberville from 1936 to 1940, and served as reeve of the Rural Municipality of Assiniboia for seven years.

Mr. Lamont was for many years a member of Westminster United Church, a member of the St. Andrew's Society, the Caledonia Society, and the Maritime Provinces Association.

He m. May Bastin, daughter of C.E. Bastin, who was also a barrister in Winnipeg. They had issue:
D1. John Salmon, 1923–1923.
D2. Mary Lamont, a retired lawyer in Winnipeg, m. Robert Mitchell, with issue:
E1. James Mitchell, m. Margaret Affleck, living in Ottawa, with issue:
F1. John Mitchell.
F2. David Mitchell.
E2. Gordon Mitchell, m. Pamela Futer, living in Powell River, B.C., with issue:
F1. Thomas Mitchell.
F2. Michael Mitchell.
F3. Mary Mitchell.
E3. Catherine Mitchell, living in Toronto.
D3. John Salmon Lamont, a prominent lawyer in Winnipeg, m. Evelyne Anderson, with issue:
E1. Andrew Lamont, living in Winnipeg.
E2. Madeleine Lamont, m. George Lennox, living in Toronto, with issue:
F1. Mariah Lennox.
E3. Maria Lamont, living in Toronto.
D4. Catherine Jean Lamont, m. Norman Pycock, living near Montreal, with issue:
E1. Catherine Pycock, living in Montreal.
E2. Jane Pycock, m. Gabriel Kassar, Saint Nicolas, Quebec, with issue:

F1. Laura Pycock-Kassar.
F2. Julia Pycock-Kassar.
E3. Elizabeth Pycock, living in Montreal.
D5. Charles Edward Lamont, 1930–1995. A Winnipeg newspaper reporting his death states:

Charles Lamont was born April 29, 1930, in Winnipeg and spent his early years in Headingley, Manitoba. He attended Laura Secord and Gordon Bell High School, where he served on the Student Council. He operated the family farm in Plumas, worked in construction in Canada's North Country and on the St. Lawrence Seaway, before returning to United College to further his education. He completed his Bachelor of Science in Mechanical Engineering in 1960 and was elected Senior Stick in his final year. His professional career included periods with Canada Packers, Fleming Pedlar and Aerofoam Chemicals before founding Controlled Environment and later Enconaire Ecological Systems. He devoted his life to the development of environmentally controlled systems for plant growth and scientific research.

His products are in operation throughout North America, Europe, Africa and Asia and he was recognized as a leading designer of sophisticated environmental equipment.

He was an active athlete when young and was chosen for the Winnipeg All-Star football team in 1947.

He was active politically in the Wolseley area and ran as a candidate provincially on two occasions. He supported children's athletic and cultural endeavours by serving as a hockey coach, Cub leader and on the Board of the Laura Secord Community Club.

He married Catherine Shearer, with issue
E1. Mary Lamont, m. Terry Shaver, Stonewall, Manitoba.

E2. Catherine Lamont, m. Douglas Makaroff, living in Victoria, B.C., with issue:
　F1. Christine Makaroff.
　F2. Michael Makaroff.
　F3. Jonathan Makaroff.
　E3. Edward Lamont, living in London, England.
D6. Francis Bastin Lamont, won a Rhodes Scholarship to study in Oxford University, England, m. Judith Barrett. *The Manitoba Law Society–Publications*, carried this item:

Francis Bastin Lamont. Died on November 13, 1998 at the age of 65. Mr. Lamont was called to the Bar in June, 1960. He articled with the firm of Thorvaldson, Eggertson, Bastin and Stringer from 1960 to 1963, when he joined James Richardson & Sons (later Richardson Securities of Canada). There, his career spanned over 25 years, starting as their one-man legal department, later rising to spend eight years as Chief Executive Officer.

After Richardson's, Mr. Lamont worked as CEO of the Saskatchewan Investment Corporation in Regina from 1988 to 1990, launching that corporation with great success. Mr. Lamont returned to Winnipeg, where he was active in specialized consulting in law and economics, largely in securities and finance.

　Francis Bastin and Judith's children are:
　　E1. John Lamont, living in Oxford, England.
　　E2. Alexandra Lamont, living in Winnipeg.
　　E3. Dougald Lamont, m. Cecelia _____, living in Winnipeg, with issue:
　　　F1. Frances Lamont.
　　E4. Laura Lamont, m. Michael Kirkland.
C3. Elizabeth Lamont, 1887–1973, m. Alexander Mutch, 1882–1958, Charlottetown, with issue:

D1. Cecilia Mutch, m. Ted Blatch, Charlottetown, with issue:
    E1. Allan Blatch.
    E2. John Blatch.
    E3. Philip Blatch.
C4. Chester Ronald Lamont lived in Winnipeg, Manitoba, never married.
C5. Preston Lamont, 1894–1894.
C6. Elvira Elsie Lamont (Veda), 1897–1990, a nurse in New York, retired to Charlottetown, never married, buried in the People's Cemetery, Charlottetown.

John Lamont

A6. John Lamont, 1812-1896, son of Malcolm Lamont and Elizabeth MacDonald, was born in the Isle of Skye, emigrated to Prince Edward Island with his parents in 1829 and took up 50 acres of land near his parents' farm in what was later called Lyndale.

He married 1) Euphemia MacLeod, a relative of the (Joiner) MacLeods who settled in Kinross. She died at the birth of her first child and he married 2) Sarah Lamont, 1833-1904, from Grandview. She was a daughter of John Lamont and Euphemia MacLeod, relatives of the Lamonts who settled in Belfast, P.E.I., in 1803, and therefore not a relative. In 1854 Sarah's parents, along with several families from the area, decided to move to the Huron County area in Ontario, where a large tract of land, called the Queen's Bush, was made available for settlement. John and Sarah also moved and took up land next to her parents. They had issue:
    B1. Margaret Lamont, b. 1852, m. James Taggert.
    B2. Euphemia Lamont, 1854-1946, m. John Taylor.
    B3. Malcolm Lamont, 1856-1942, m. 1) Elizabeth Ann Tervit, 2) Jane Long (Jennie).

Above: Malcolm Lamont and Ann Tervit with their children, Pearl and George.
Below: Malcolm Lamont and Jennie Long

B4. Sarah Lamont, 1858-1918, m. John Colling.
B5. Angus Charles Lamont, 1860-1923, m. 1) Edith Violet Hagen, 2) Lillian Virginia Hagen, 3) Anna Sophia Ansonen.

B6. Elizabeth Lamont, 1862-1934.
B7. Catherine Lamont, 1864-1891, m. John McNamara.
B8. John Gordon Lamont, b. 1869 or 1870.
B9. Catherine Lamont (Carrie), 1873-1894, m. Arthur Lee Hamilton.[1]

John and Sarah are both buried in the Wingham Cemetery. The following obituaries appeared in a local paper:

The Wingham Times
September 4, 1896

On Wednesday, John Lamont, who lived with his son, M.B. Lamont, Patrick Street, passed away at the ripe age of 84 years and three months. Mr. Lamont was a native of Invernesshire, Scotland and came to Cape Breton [should read Prince Edward Island] when 18 years of age where he lived for twenty-five years. In 1855 he came to Huron County, Turnberry, living on that farm until two years ago when his son, M.B., sold the old homestead and moved into Wingham.

He had a large family—three sons and six daughters—all of whom are living. They are:

M.B.; Angus of Chicago; Dr. J. G. of Cando, North Dakota, Mrs. Taggert of Michigan; Mrs. Taylor, Ripley; Mrs. A. Hamilton, Palmerston, Mrs. MacNamara, Dobbington; Miss Sadie, Ripley and Miss Lizzie, of town (Wingham). The funeral which is private will take place today. Mr. Lamont was always a man of retiring disposition and never cared to take an active part in public affairs. He was a Presbyterian and a Liberal in politics. He was temperate in all his habits and to this may be attributed his long lease of life.

---

1   The publisher is indebted to Pat Lamont's book, *Scots on the Move* (2009), found among Harold MacLeod's papers, for the list of John and Sarah Lamont's offspring.

The Lamonts of Lyndale

The Wingham Times
April 28, 1904

There died at Ripley on Saturday morning last, a former well known resident of this section in the person of Mrs. S. Lamont, aged 70 years. Deceased was born in Prince Edward Island and many years ago moved into Turnberry settling with her husband on the farm near Zetland now owned by Mr. W.J. Deyell. After residing on the farm for a number of years Mrs. Lamont lived for some time at Zetland and over twenty years ago moved to Ripley where she has since resided. She had not been ill for long, having been seized with a stroke of paralysis on the Tuesday previous to her death. Mrs. Lamont was held in high esteem by all who knew her and she will be remembered by many of the older residents of this section. Deceased was the mother of nine children all of whom are surviving viz: Mrs. John Taggert, Michigan; Mrs. MacNamarra, Paisley; Miss Lizzie Lamont, Winnipeg; Miss Sarah Lamont, Ripley; Mrs. John Taylor and Mrs. A.L. Hamilton, Wingham; Dr. John Lamont, Canda, North Dakota; Angus Lamont, Michigan; Malcolm Lamont, Wingham. The remains were brought to Wingham on Tuesday afternoon, the funeral taking place from the G.T.R. station to the Wingham cemetery. All the members of the family were present at the funeral except Mrs. Taggert and Angus Lamont.

Ewen Lamont

A7. Ewen Lamont, 1817-1905, son of Malcolm Lamont and Elizabeth MacDonald, was born in Bernisdale, Isle of Skye, came to this country in 1829 with his parents and settled first near Vernon River on land lately in possession of Wendell Drake. A short time later they moved to Orwell Head, later called Lyndale, to be near the Rev. Donald MacDonald who had a preaching station at what was known as Orwell Head Church. Ewen was a school teacher, a hymn writer, a poet and a writer of wills. He was ordained an Elder by the Rev. Donald MacDonald and was a lay preacher after the death of Mr. MacDonald, baptizing a number of children. He was an excellent singer. The minister MacDonald, at one time, had him ejected from his seat with the Elders because he voted at a general election, contrary to the minister's wishes. At that time the Elders sat at the front of the church and facing the people. With Ewen missing there was a lack in the singing. The minister was forced to re-instate him with the words: "Come up here Ewen, let no man take your crown."

When he had written his first hymn, he took it to the Rev. Donald MacDonald for approval. The minister looked it over, all 21 verses, and told him it was "too long, much too long, but let me hear you sing a verse or two." Ewen sang two verses and the minister motioned him to continue. After Ewen sang all of the verses, the minister stated emphatically, "its too short, much too short."

Malcolm MacQueen, in his book *Skye Pioneers*, writes:

> Rev. Samuel Angus Martin, now of Manitoba, recalls the occasion when, as a young man, he heard the debate between the elders of the Murray Harbour Road church as to whether Cook's Helps should be introduced into the Sunday school.
>
> Mr. William MacPhail spoke in favour of the innovation. Ewen Lamont, a local preacher, arose and condemned the proposal. He made a speech filled with deep emotion. Finally, taking one of the pamphlets in his hands, and holding it aloft, he exclaimed with great feeling as he tore it asunder. "This is the human help to aid the Bible you would introduce into the Sunday school."

In the March 1875 *Monthly Record of The Church of Scotland*, we find a letter dated January 25th, 1875, and written by Rev. P. Melville, who was minister of the church in Georgetown, P.E.I. The following excerpts are from that letter:

Dear Mr. Editor:

Long will the year 1874 be memorable in our town, and in our Isle, as "the year of the revival," or rather as the beginning of the revival. It was the third year of my charge in this Parish, our most anxious year, and our most successful by far. Well may we raise our Ebenezer here, and gratefully own that "Hitherto hath the Lord helped us!" ...

The great revival visitation in Georgetown began in March, 1874. ... We assembled every evening in the church for prayer. Night after night the meetings were so large that we dared not give them up. Still we had a hard struggle. We prayed for revival but the spirit of prayer appeared to withhold. We waited and toiled long, and almost to despair. We asked help of more favoured congregations in vain. We were in extreme danger of giving up hope, and effort too, when the dear destitute church at Orwell Head heard our cry, and at once sent two of their choicest Elders to our aid, Messrs. Ewen Lamont and William MacPhail [father of Sir Andrew MacPhail]. That very night, while they prayed with us, we saw the sign of revival. Though it was but as a little cloud like a man's hand rising from the sea of Divine grace to the brazen sky of human despair, yet the word was spoken, "Behold he prayeth!" Others followed quickly after, and from that night forward, the drops fell from heaven until the clouds became so heavy as to be awful. Many cried out in terror and in tears, "Is there mercy yet for me? O Lord deliver my soul, I beseech thee!" Then the Lord's handmaids came up to help with His servants, and trampled the fear of man under foot. Scoffers shut their mouth in awe. Young men and maidens, old folks and children, boldly testified for Jesus, and joined publicly in His service. Who can ever forget those days and nights of spiritual travail? Who can ever forget the Lord's mercy in our extremity? Who can ever forget the dear people who came to our aid, though without a minister themselves.

After the death of Rev. Donald MacDonald, the Rev. James MacColl served in the parish for about three years before going back to Scotland.

Finally, in 1874 a call was placed in the hands of Rev. John Goodwill who was born in Nova Scotia, and had spent some time doing missionary work among the natives of the South Sea Islands.

He accepted the call, but he had learned the Gaelic language when older and the Gaelic speaking people found him difficult to follow. He was also bitterly opposed to liquor and tobacco when most of the elders used both.

Anyone smoking, he said was "burning incense to the devil." The elders used to kiss the Minister MacDonald. When one of their number in Orwell Head attempted the same on Goodwill, he shouted at him, "Keep away, you smell of tobacco." Needless to say, there were no more attempts in that direction by any of the other elders.

It was said that he had a weak stomach which left him irritable. One of Charles MacLeod's children was sick, and since the child was not baptized, he went after Rev. Goodwill to perform the rite. It was winter, the weather was contrary. According to Charles, the minister growled and snapped at him all the way to the home and back, for not having the child baptized when the weather was more pleasant.

This was in sharp contrast to the Rev. Donald MacDonald whom Principal Leitch, of Queen's University, described as a "hearty hilarious man with a keen appreciation of the humorous." A lady from O'Leary, in relating her first remembrance of seeing MacDonald stated that: "When we first caught sight of him walking toward our home, the children, in great excitement, all ran to meet him, and I remember yet how they all walked up the lane together, he had one child in his arms and another on his shoulders while holding the hand of another and all talking and laughing together."

Things finally came to a head and a number from the Eastern section of the parish left the Goodwill camp to form their own group, under the name of MacDonaldites. John Compton from Belle River, and George Bears from Brooklyn were appointed ministering elders with Ewen Lamont as ministering elder to the Gaelic members and adherents. Ewen, along with six families from the immediate area, held services in his home for a number of years until word was brought to him that a revival had begun under Rev. Goodwill, when he was preaching in DeSable Church.

Ewen's response was: "The Lord's hand is on Mr. Goodwill, we will fully support him, we will have no more services here."

There were two revivals during the pioneer Rev. Donald MacDonald's ministry on P.E.I., and some time before his death in 1867, he stated to his elders that another revival would occur following his own death.

This letter gives an account of the beginning of this revival which later spread throughout all the churches which had been built under his ministry. Michael MacLeod, Point Prim, was one of a large number of elders ordained by Mr. MacDonald, and John MacEachern was a fellow elder from Cherry Valley, from where he writes to Michael regarding the church.

The parish was divided by the Hillsborough River, which was crossed on a ferry, hence the reference in the letter to the other side.

Cherry Valley, Dec. 17, 1891
Mr. Michael MacLeod

My Dear Sir,

I have no doubt you have heard an account of the Revival now going on in Rev. Mr. Goodwill's church at DeSable and the other churches under his charge. You will be pleased and no doubt surprised to hear that in extent and numbers it far exceeds the last revival under the late Mr. MacDonald's ministry.

Last Sabbath being Mr. Goodwill's day at Birch Hill, he was unable to leave the people on the other side but sent two elders instead to hold meetings for a few days with us.

In their account of the revival. They say they are amazed at the power with which he preaches the Word, and the extent of the awakening especially among the young children from eight years and upward, crying for mercy.

The church at DeSable is packed full every night, all in motion, some in one stage and some in another, all apparently brought under the influence of the Spirit of God.

The movement is not confined to our people alone, but numbers from other churches are brought under the influence of the Spirit. I will mention one case, a woman belonging to another church did not wish her family to be going, but could not keep them away.

The mother followed and when she came into the church and saw her daughters among the rest under the Power, such as you have seen at former revivals, she stood for some time looking at them, when she broke down and was brought under the influence of the same Spirit.

It is Mr. Goodwill's desire and prayer that the revival may extend to this side also. We are praying that this side may not be passed by when there is such an outpouring of the Spirit on the other side.

May God bless yourself, wife and family, is the sincere desire of your friend.

John MacEachern

The elder's prayers were answered, the revival swept over the Eastern Parish with a greater intensity than was seen in MacDonald's time.

Ewen, who had published a brief sketch of the life of MacDonald [found at the end of this book], writing from Lyndale, P.E.I., in March 1892, stated: "I have briefly recorded some incidents of the past, concerning that notable revival of religion that began over sixty years ago on this Island under the ministry of the late Rev. Donald MacDonald, of which I was an eye witness. Now in my old age, it is my happy lot to be an eye witness to another remarkable revival, begun a few months ago, under the ministry of the Rev. John Goodwill, and which I believe to be essentially the same as the other two revivals referred to in my 'Sketch,' if not more powerful in its influence and more rapid in its progress; many hundreds, old and young, and of different nationalities and sects being affected already by it."

Ewen took over his parents' farm and in 1870 added to it 50 acres purchased from Murdoch and Ann Bruce, son of Malcolm Bruce. The Bruce family moved to the Nebraska territory, where free land was opened up by the United States Government for settlement. The purchase of this property gave Ewen access to a flowing brook as well as a good rising spring of water.

Ewen was a good craftsman. He made a set of bagpipes which Murdock and Donald used to play at various community gatherings. However, the bagpipes came to a sad end. A horse belonging to William Gillis, their neighbour, broke out of the pasture and into Ewen's grain field. Murdock, in attempting to remove the animal, picked up the nearest object which was an axe and threw it at the horse. The axe landed blade first with the result of a bad cut on the horse's front leg. Ewen blamed the accident on the bagpipes and immediately burned them. He thought the boys were wasting time with the pipes when they should be attending to the needs of the farm.

When the Lamonts purchased the original property in Lyndale. They built the house and barn not far from the Lyndale road. In later years, Ewen moved the buildings farther back to a hill in the center of the farm and with a better view of the countryside.

He moved the house first without difficulty, but when moving the barn it collapsed before reaching its destination. He was then forced to build a new barn.

About 1895, Murdock (Ewen's son), who was then operating the farm with Ewen and Sarah living in part of the house, sold the farm to Murdock Bruce, a neighbour, and moved to Stanchel near his sister Frances. His brother Angus moved to that area as well, selling his farm to John Henry MacLeod.

Neither brother were farming very long in Stanchel before Murdock moved to Massachusetts where he worked at the carpentry trade before studying for the ministry. Angus moved to Sydney, Nova Scotia, where he was a merchant.

According to his neighbours, Ewen was a happy man, quick witted and always ready to laugh. His family, as well, inherited that carefree attitude, that ability to see the humour in almost any situation. They would always greet you with a smile and were ever ready to overlook the frailties of human nature.

Ewen's obituary in a local paper reads:

> One of the old pioneers of this Island passed off the stage of time on October 26th, 1905, in the person of Ewen Lamont, Esq. He was born in the Isle of Skye in the year 1817 and emigrated to this Island in the year 1830. For over 40 years he was in the teaching profession in different parts of the Island. He lived in Lyndale until about 11 years ago when he moved to Stanchel.
>
> Early in life he was brought to a knowledge of the truth under the ministry of the late Rev. Donald MacDonald, by whom he was ordained an Elder in the Church of Jesus Christ, an office the duties of which were faithfully per-

formed by him. He was also a poet of no mean order, and many of his spiritual songs are still sung in the churches and are remarkable for their deep spiritual experiences.

The welfare of the church was ever in his mind, and during his lingering sickness he showed the power of the religion of Jesus Christ to sustain the inward man whilst the outward man is gradually declining. It is now fulfilled in his own experience, the sentiments expressed in one of his hymns:

> *The Kingdom of glory we then shall inherit,*
> *The house of our Father, where pleasures abound,*
> *The home that we neither could purchase nor merit,*
> *Where aught that defileth shall never be found*
> *Where we shall see Jesus and worship before Him*
> *And where His beloved shall ever abide.*
> *Where ransomed millions shall praise and adore Him*
> *When he shall rejoice in His glorified Bride.*

In a letter to the Charlottetown *Guardian* in 1952, Mr. M. MacKenzie, from Canoe Cove, P.E.I., wrote:

> Sir,–In your issue of the 13th of last November, there appeared in the Forum, a letter written by W.D. Lamont of Glasgow, Scotland, pointing out to members of the Lamont family living on Prince Edward Island, that they could claim on her maternal side a blood relationship to Princess Elizabeth, whose recent visit to us still lingers as a happy memory for us all. It is for me, however, a sad comment in connection to this letter to have to say that one branch of this family, like branches of other noted families, has almost completely vanished from our Island. I refer here to the Lamonts of Orwell.
>
> Older residents of our island, like myself, who know some-

thing of the record of the Lamonts at home and abroad will, I judge, feel that their relationship to our present Queen is a credit to both parties concerned. For example of this record, we have only to recall that a few years ago it was announced in the *Guardian* that a son of Murdoch Lamont of Glasgow, formerly of Prince Edward Island, was appointed as British adviser to the Egyptian Government and one that only a man of great learning and dignity could properly fulfill. In the brief report of this appointment that appeared in the *Guardian* Mr. Lamont was mentioned as a brilliant Oxford student and winner of an Oxford scholarship: and it was also stated that his father before his son's college days had been a brilliant and outstanding student in arts and theology at Edinburgh University, winning a prize there that was open to students from every approved college in the British Empire. The Rev. Murdoch Lamont too, was mentioned as a brother of the late Rev. Donald Lamont, one time minister in the Central Parish of the Prince Edward Island Church of Scotland, now a parish in the Presbyterian Church of Canada. He was the author of two books on religious topics, viz.: *Seven Great Questions,* and *Where are Our Dead?*

Both of these ministers were sons of the late Ewen Lamont of Orwell, one of the more distinguished persons mentioned, by the way, in Malcolm MacQueen's *Skye Pioneers.* He was by profession both a farmer and public school teacher, and was considered in his own day to be a splendid English and Gaelic scholar, with a strong bent for religious poetry. He was a loyal follower of the Scottish Pioneer minister and evangelist, Rev. Donald MacDonald, and wrote a brief sketch of his minister's life which was published and widely read, among the descendants of the minister's first followers, about sixty years ago, that is to say about thirty years after the minister's death …

Ewen married Sarah MacPherson, 1827-1911, daughter of

John MacPherson and Mary Currie, from Little Sands. Ewen couldn't have picked a better partner. Since he was away a lot of the time teaching, it fell on her to look after the demands of the farm. She was a strong, efficient woman.

Sarah MacPherson and Ewen Lamont

She sheared the sheep, she washed the wool, she butchered a lamb to provide meat for the table, and would oversee the sowing and reaping of the farm crops.

After his death, she kept his hat hanging on her bedpost and when one of her daughters removed it, during Spring housecleaning, she demanded that it be put back without delay and not to be touched in future, under any circumstances.

She remained in her home up to the time of her death even though her daughters tried to persuade her to live with one of them.

At one time, Rebecca and Frances decided that the time had come for her to be moved, forcibly if not otherwise. Rebecca volunteered to go and tell her what they had planned. She walked through the fields from Frances' home and when she reached her mother's house she had to climb over a fence; suddenly she heard a voice, loud and clear, stating: "The walls of Jerusalem must be built."

Rebecca took this as a warning not to interfere with her mother's living arrangement and, consequently, couldn't mention moving to her mother.

A Charlottetown newspaper reported the death of Sarah as follows:

> The old landmarks of P.E.I. are fast passing away. The past winter has removed many of them, and on April 27th another of the well known and highly respected inhabitants of Stanchel was called to her everlasting home. Mrs. Ewen Lamont (nee Sarah MacPherson) had seen great changes take place in her Island home during the eighty-four years of her pilgrimage. Early in life she had heard the voice "Awake thou that sleepest, arise from the dead and Christ shall give thee light" and was brought to the consciousness of sins forgiven through the blood of a crucified Saviour
>
> She lived and died in the full assurance of a happier life beyond the grave. Although only nine days laid aside from the active duties of life, she was anxiously looking forward to a final victory …

Ewen Lamont and Sarah MacPherson had the following family:

B1. Frances Lamont, 1845-1937, m. Alexander MacIntosh, 1846-1917, from Stanchel, P.E.I. They moved to Strathmore, Alberta, in 1917, to be near their sons. He is buried in Union Cemetery, Calgary, Alberta, and after his death she came back to P.E.I. She died at the home of her daughter, Rebecca Banks, in the Annapolis Valley. Her remains were taken back to Stanchel where the funeral was held from the home of Jim Todd, with burial in Springton cemeter

Alexander MacIntosh and Frances Lamont in Alberta, shortly before Alexander's death.

A Calgary paper printed the following:

Alexander MacIntosh, who came from Stanchel, P.E.I., four months ago to live in the Cheadle District near the home of his son, Robert (Richard) MacIntosh, died in the

General Hospital on Saturday night as the result of an operation performed three days previous.

Deceased is survived by three daughters: Mrs. F. King of Pugwash, Nova Scotia, Mrs. John Banks and Mrs. Thomas of Boston, and three sons: J.A. MacIntosh, of Three Hills, Alberta; Donald MacIntosh, of Stanchel, P.E.I., and Robert MacIntosh, of Cheadle, Alberta.

The funeral was held at 2 o'clock this afternoon from Harrison and Foster's undertaking parlours.

Frances, before her marriage, worked in the Boston area. Below is a copy of a letter from her employer, addressed to her father:

Quincy Street
Cambridge, Mass.
Mr. Lamont
September, 1865.

My Dear Sir:

We are unwilling that your daughter Frances should go home without carrying from us some testimonial of the very high regard in which we hold her. Modest, gentle, kind and faithful, we have found in her nothing to blame but everything to praise. She has deserved everything good that we can say of her and do for her. We have esteemed her as if she were a member of our own family. We have been married over thirty years and my wife and I have agreed that we never had a girl that we liked as well as we do Frances and we hope that a kind Providence will relieve your anxiety on her account.

My wife and daughters send their affectionate regards to you and Mrs. Lamont.

I am yours truly
A.P. Peabody

On Frances's 90th birthday a Charlottetown newspaper reported that she holds the proud distinction of being a great-great-grandmother. Her descendants are as follows: Her daughter, Mrs. James Thomas, Brighton, Mass.; her granddaughter, Mrs. Sydney Taylor, Winsloe; her great-grand daughter, Mrs. Hurry, of Highfield; and her great-great-grandchild, baby Hurry, making five living generations, something unique in the province of Prince Edward Island.

Sir Andrew MacPhail in his book *The Master's Wife*, tells of Frances visiting his home:

> In the summer of 1930, the daughter of this elder [Ewen Lamont] spent some days with us. She was slight and beautiful as a wraith, and being eighty-six years old, her voice was suitably thin for the pure melody. She sang in Gaelic and English the hymns her father had written nearly a hundred years ago; for he wrote them the year he was "set free." Three years later, she came again, but old age had done its work, as it has done with even more famous singer.

The children of Frances Lamont and Alexander MacIntosh are:

>C1. Christine Frances MacIntosh, 1872-1893, m. James Alfred Thomas, 1870-1947, Christine died after the birth of her second daughter, on Dec. 19th, 1893, at age 21. On her deathbed she asked her sister Margaret to take care of her children. Margaret married the father and had nine more children by him. Christine's children were:
>>D1. Mary Elizabeth Thomas (Libby), b. 1892, m. Sidney Taylor, son of Capt. William Taylor, Millview. They farmed in Vernon and later went to

Alberta about 1918.

An item that appeared in a local paper at the time reads:

Mr. Sydney Taylor, who recently sold his farm at Vernon left Thursday for Western Canada accompanied by his family. Other farmers who left the Island the same day for the West are: Mr. Augustine Brothers, Sparrow's Road, Mr. Alexander Drake, Millview, who sold his farm to his brother Pearl Drake, and Mr. William Drake and wife of Millview. Those are industrious and progressive farmers. Their departure means a considerable loss to this Province. Meanwhile the best wishes for happiness and prosperity for those citizens in their new homes from a large circle of friends are hereby extended.

The Taylors farmed for a few years in Western Canada, before returning to P.E.I. and farming in Winsloe. They had issue:

E1. Margaret Elizabeth Taylor, m. Charles Hurry. They lived in Highfield, P.E.I., and had issue:
F1. Sidney Charles Hurry, m. Beryl Gertrude Easter. They live in Winsloe and had issue:
G1. Paul Sidney Hurry, m. Gail Adams, with issue:
H1. Lacey Hurry.
H2. Jessie Hurry.
G2. Anne Lorraine Hurry, m. James Johnson, with issue:
H1. Olivia Johnson.
G3. Carolyn Gertrude Hurry, m. David Byck, with issue:
H1. Alexandra Byck.
H2. Shawn Byck.

G4. David Charles Hurry, m. Shelly Smith, with issue:
    H1. Davin Hurry.
F2. Audrey Elizabeth Hurry, m. Leslie Willard MacPhail, with issue:
    G1. Leslie Alan MacPhail, m. Linda Beaton, issue:
        H1. Brandon Alan MacPhail.
        H2. Sarah MacPhail.
    G2. Carol Elizabeth MacPhail, m. Michael Wark, with issue:
        H1. Michelle Wark.
        H2. Catlyn Wark.
        H3. Jonathan Wark.
    G3. Kenneth Charles MacPhail, m. Debby Upton, with issue:
        H1. Angela MacPhail.
        H2. Adam MacPhail.
        H3. Mathew MacPhail.
    G4. Virginia Louise MacPhail, m. Terry MacEachern. With issue:
        H1. Stephanie MacEachern.
        H2. Lindsay MacEachern.
        H3. Mark MacEachern.
    G5. John Wayne MacPhail, m. Joan Green, with issue:
        H1. Erin MacPhail.
        H2. Ellen MacPhail.
    G6. Shelly Rotha MacPhail, m. Robert Burns, with issue:
        H1. Robert Burns.
        H2. Richelle Burns.
F3. Lorna Jeanine Hurry, m. Arthur Blair Wheatly, Warren Grove, with issue:
    G1. Marlene Lorna Wheatly, m. Norman

Scott, with issue:
- H1. Mary Ann Scott.
- H2. Peter Scott.
- H3. Julia Scott.

G2. Nancy Elizabeth Wheatly, m. Ralph Freeze. They live in Western Canada, with issue:
- H1. Emily Elizabeth Freeze.
- H2. Rebecca Freeze.
- H3. Jillian Freeze.

G3. Gordon Arthur Wheatly, m. Jackie Barry, with issue:
- H1. Taylor Wheatly.
- H2. Dillon Wheatly.
- H3. Sydney Wheatly.

F4. Miriam Roberta Hurry, m. Gordon Francis Love, with issue:
- G1. Lorelei Margaret Love.
- G2. Donna Maureen Love, m. Peter Dawes, with issue:
  - H1. Alexandra Dawes.
  - H2. Troy Dawes.
- G3. Noreen Roberta Love, m. Nelson Letts, with issue:
  - H1. Alexis Letts.

F5. Frances Carolyn Hurry, m. Ross Albert Lewis, issue:
- G1. Colby Chadburn Lewis, m. Lori Anne Proud, with issue:
  - H1. Thomas Charles Lewis.
  - H2. Jodi Mae Lewis.
  - H3. Morgan Harrison Lewis.
  - H4. Katelyn Brittney Lewis.
  - H5. Sydney Carolyn Lewis.
- G2. Melanie Jean Lewis, m. Ronald Babi-

neau.

G3. Margaret Elizabeth Lewis, m. Myron Franklin MacDonald, with issue:

H1. Jackson Franklin MacDonald.

H2. Jenna Elizabeth MacDonald.

E2. Hazel Adelaid Taylor, 1915–1989, daughter of Sidney Taylor and Libby Thomas, m. David Leroy Walker, 1914–1978. They lived in New Annan, P.E.I., with issue:

F1. Margaret Elizabeth Walker, m. Irving Boswell, Marshfield, P.E.I., with issue:

G1. Christine Lothian, m. Wayne Mearns with issue:

H1. Jerad Wayne Mearns.

H2. Heath Donald Mearns.

H3. Holt MacKenzie Mearns.

G2. Brenda Boswell, m. Hughie James MacDonald, from Freeland, Lot 11, P.E.I., with issue:

H1. Sarah Elizabeth MacDonald and Allan Millar, with issue:

I1. Jamin Glen Irving MacDonald.

H2. Justin Hughie MacDonald.

G3. Irving Lorne Boswell, m. Cindy Wilbert, issue:

H1. Matthew David Boswell.

H2. Nicholas Jay Boswell.

H3. Christopher John Boswell.

G4. Sheila Blanche Boswell, m. Leonard Marshall, with issue:

H1. Allyson Marshall.

H2. Ashley Marshall.

H3. Jason Marshall.

F2. David Sidney Walker, m. Anne Shirley Morrison, with issue:

G1. Debra Catherine Walker, m. Gary Edgar Raymond. They live in Yarmouth, N.S., with issue:
    H1. Kaitlyn Ruth Raymond.
    H2. Graeme Edgar Douglas Raymond.
    H3. Emmalee Anne Raymond.
    H4. Scott David Raymond.
G2. David Brian Walker, living in Comox, B.C., m. 1) Sandra Henwood, with issue:
    H1. Andrew David Walker.
    H2. Kory Justin Walker.
    H3. Brodie William Walker.
    H4. Troy Dillion Walker.
David m. 2) Angela Pownall.
G3. Patricia Rae Walker, m. Mark MacFadzen, living in Fredericton, N.B., with issue:
    H1. Tyler Mark MacFadzen.
    H2. Jessie Anne MacFadzen.
G4. Peter Wayne Walker, m. Barbara Anne Johnstone, with issue:
    H1. Andrea Shirley Walker.
    H2. Sarah Elizabeth Walker.
G5. Janice Adelaide Walker, m. David Ralph Hogg, with issue:
    H1. Timothy David Hogg.
    H2. Charlotte Anne Hogg.
F3. Joan Deborah Walker, m. Jason Glover, from Kelvin Grove, P.E.I., with issue:
    G1. Cindy Lou Glover, m. Ronald Black, with issue:
        H1. Matthew Black.
        H2. Jenna Black.
    G2. Deborah Anne Glover, m. Bjorn Andreason, with issue:

H1. Amber Andreason, m. Robert Crozier, Winsloe, P.E.I.
H2. Starla Andreason.
G3. Michael Glover, m. Joan Madson, with issue:
H1. Kara Glover.
H2. Kyle Glover.
G4. Stephen Paul Glover, m. Manon Turcotte, with issue:
H1. Danielle Anne Glover.
H2. Travis Stephen Glover.
F4. Edwin Winston Walker, m. Pauline MacCallum, New Annan, with issue:
G1. Sharon Lynn Walker.
G2. Kimberly Anne Walker, m. Paul Stephen Bonner, from England.
E3. Myrtle Alberta Taylor, daughter of Sidney Taylor and Libby Thomas, m. Cedric Ballem. They lived in Marshfield, with issue:
F1. Evelyn Elizabeth Ballem, m. Douglas Blair MacDonald, with issue:
G1. Robert James MacDonald, m. Judith Helene Gauthier, with issue:
H1. Catherine Helene MacDonald.
H2. Alexander MacDonald (Sandy).
H3. Carolyn MacDonald.
G2. Wendy Elizabeth MacDonald, m. Jacob Skinner (Jake).
G3. Brian Douglas MacDonald.
F2. Myrna Belle Ballem, m. Robert Carlyle Sanderson, with issue:
G1. Angela Lynne Sanderson, m. Brent Irving, issue:
H1. Brodie Sanderson Irving.
H2. Amanda Irving.

G2. Jody John Sanderson.
G3. Kathy Diane Sanderson.
G4. Marcia Helen Sanderson.
F3. Marsha Lynne Ballem, m. Dan Russell Proude, with issue:
G1. Gordon Russell Proude.
G2. Patricia Dawn Proude, m. 1) Charles Roggeveen, with issue:
H1. Kees Charles Roggeveen.
Patricia m. 2) Stephen Murley, with issue:
H2. Damon Chad Murley.
G3. Gregory Owen Proude, m. Kimberly Peters, with issue:
H1. Kristen Rae Proude.
F4. Linda Pauline Ballem, m. Stephen Bernard MacDonald, with issue:
G1. Stephen Troy MacDonald, m. April Squarebriggs, with issue:
H1. Alexander MacDonald.
G2. Timothy John MacDonald, m. Joelle Gildert.
G3. Kelli Joan MacDonald, m. Mike Profitt, with issue:
H1. Drew Profitt.
H2. Emma Profitt.
H3. Nicolas Profitt.
G4. Andrew William Cedric MacDonald.
G5. Rebecca JoAnne MacDonald.
G6. Jennifer Grace MacDonald.
F5. James Wayne Ballem, m. 1) Yvone Catherine Murray, with issue:
G1. Joshua William Ballem.
G2. Jarrod Wayne Ballem.
James m. 2) Cynthia E. MacLean.
F6. John Charles Ballem, m. Anna Marie

Nolan, with issue:
  G1. Christopher Gordon Ballem.
  G2. Carolyn Jane Ballem.
  G3. Michael Ivan Ballem.
E4. Cecil Perley Taylor, son of Sidney Taylor and Libby Thomas, m. Dorothy MacDonald. They farmed in Winsloe, later moved to Charlottetown. They had issue:
  F1. Alan Cecil Taylor, was a school teacher in Charlottetown, m. 1) Phyllis Mary Jane MacMillan, with issue:
    G1. David Taylor, died in infancy.
    G2. Cathy Lynn Taylor.
    G3. Krista Taylor.
  Alan married 2) Barbara Trainor, living in Charlottetown.
  F2. Elizabeth Anne Taylor, m. Gordon William Long. They live in Charlottetown, with issue:
    G1. Maureen Elizabeth Long.
    G2. Christina Louise Long.
    G3. Sharon Mary-Lee Long.
  F3. Heather Ruth Taylor, m. Robert Hill. They live in Ottawa, with issue:
    G1. Andrew Taylor Hill.
    G2. David Hill.
  F4. Eleanor Louise Taylor, m. Martin Jost Kreplin, Ottawa. They had issue:
    G1. Sarah Lynn Kreplin.
    G2. Matthew West Kreplin.
D2. Christina Thomas, 1893–1981, daughter of Christine MacIntosh and James Thomas, m. James Robert Todd, 1888-1964, Stanchel, P.E.I., with issue:
  E1. Samuel Robert Todd, 1913-1915.

E2. James Ewen Todd, 1915–2002, m. Rita Frizzell, 1923-1998. They lived in Stanchel, later moved to Charlottetown, and had a boy and a girl:
    F1. Kelsie Murray Todd, m. Debby Sweet, living in Charlottetown.
    F2. Vaunda Joan Todd, m. Edward Whalen, living in Charlottetown.

E3. Margaret Frances Todd, m. Reginald Compton, from Summerside. They had issue:
    F1. Margaret Etta Compton, m. Don Burch, living in Summerside.
    F2. Doris Elaine Compton, m. Robert Peterson, living in Oyster Bed Bridge.
    F3. Catherine Violet Compton, m. Lloyd Banks, Kensington.
    F4. Charles Reginald Compton, m. Barbara Jean Ferguson.
    F5. Leeland Grant Compton, m. Paulette Gaudet.
    F6. Albert Wayne Compton, m. Anne _____, living in St. Eleanor's.

E4. Ella Mae Todd, m. Charles Edward Sherren, from Crapaud. They had issue:
    F1. Hazel Mae Sherren, m. 1) Don Graham, 2) Troy MacDonald, living in Edmonton, Alberta.
    F2. Myron Robert Sherren, m. Wanda Isabel MacPhee, living in Sherwood.
    F3. Gordon Bell Sherren, m. Brenda Ferguson, living in Dundas, P.E.I.
    F4. Irene Rose Sherren, living in Crapaud.
    F5. James Wilfred Sherren, m. Lorna Prosser.
    F6. Charles Edward Sherren, m. Noreen Bradley.

E5. Annie Elizabeth Todd, 1919-1997, m. Ivan Lemuel Frizzell, Charlottetown, with issue:
  F1. Donald Ivan Frizzell, Charlottetown, businessman, m. Diane Hazel Jardine, from Charlottetown. They had issue:
    G1. James Donald Frizzell, m. Susan MacDonald. They live in Charlottetown, with issue:
      H1. Stephen Frizzell.
      H2. Vanessa Frizzell.
    G2. Paul William Frizzell, m. Karen Sinclair. They are living in St. John, N.B., with issue:
      H1. Jasmine Grace Frizzell.
      H2. Jenna Faith Frizzell.
  F2. Vernon Wilfred Frizzell, m. Glenda Erna Kitson, living in Charlottetown. They had issue:
    G1. Lorelei Glenda Frizzell, a pharmacist in Charlottetown, m. Paul Zakem.
    G2. Jennifer Liane Frizzell, Charlottetown.
    G3. David Vernon Frizzell, living in Toronto.
  F3. George Edison Frizzell, living in Moncton, m. Pauline Gloria Goguen, with issue:
    G1. Ronald Edward Frizzell, married in Moncton with two daughters.
    G2. Dana Lillian Frizzell, married in Moncton with two daughters.
    G3. Randy George Frizzell.
    G4. Kelly Anne Frizzell.
  F4. Lorna Mae Frizzell, m. Colin George Arthur, from Liverpool, England. They live in Red Deer, Alberta, with issue:

G1. David Bertram Arthur, m. Heather _____, with issue:
    H1. Stephen Arthur.
G2. Kimberley Anne Arthur, m. Robert Knaull, with issue:
    H1. Jessica Knaull.
    H2. Krista Knaull.
F5. Warren James Frizzell, m. Carol Marie Stanley, living in Charlottetown. They had issue:
    G1. Winnifred Angela Frizzell.
    G2. James Robert Andrew Frizzell, b. 1976.
    G3. Aaron James Frizzell.
    G4. Nicholas Frizzell.
F6. Rev. Roger Dean Frizzell, clergyman with a pastorate in New Brunswick, married Gloria MacMillan. They have three children:
    G1. Mark Dean Frizzell, m. Karen Burke, with issue:
        H1. Connor Frizzell.
        H2. Samuel Frizzell.
    G2. Helen Anne Frizzell.
    G3. Matthew James Frizzell.
F7. Daughter
E6. Catherine Jane Todd, m. Walter John Edwards, from Victoria, B.C. They had issue:
    F1. Jackie Walter Edwards, 1943-1943.
    F2. David Earl Edwards, m. Teresa Joan Brown, living in Kamloops, B.C.
    F3. Judy Ann Edwards, m. Michael Elwood, living in Kamloops, B.C.
    F4. Donna Vera Edwards, m. Brian Earl Stanley, living in Kamloops, B.C.
    F5. Norma Jean Edwards, m. Ben Derring,

living in Calgary, Alberta.
F6. Carl Robert Edwards, m. Delores _____, living in Canmore, Alberta.
F7. Joan Elaine Edwards, m. _____, Kamloops, B.C.

E7. Olive Maude Todd, 1923-1924.

E8. Violet Rebecca Todd, m. Leland Paynter Mayne, from Emerald, P.E.I. They had issue:
F1. Barry Leeland Mayne, m. Carol Joann Wallace, living in Emerald, P.E.I.
F2. Brenda Elaine Mayne, a schoolteacher, m. Wendell Sinclair, Springfield, P.E.I.
F3. Janice Catherine Mayne, 1953-1956.
F4. Alan Todd Mayne, m. Rose Affleck, living in Charlottetown.
F5. Carol Anne Mayne.
F6. James Kevin Mayne.
F7. Kenneth Trent Mayne.

E9. Hazel Christena Todd, m. Leslie Sterling Frizzell, from Stanchel. They had issue:
F1. Cecil Leslie Frizzell, m. Marion Noreen Reeves.
F2. Diane Christena Frizzell, m. Arnie Winsor, from Nfld.

E10. Daniel Earl Todd, 1931-1969, m. Lena Winchester from Summerside.
F1. James Melvin Todd.
F2. Jackie Walter Todd.
F3. Carl Robert Todd.
F4. David Earl Todd.

Daniel Earl Todd's obituary in a local paper reads:

Relatives and friends were shocked and saddened to learn of the tragic death of Daniel Earl Todd as the result of a fire in Hamilton Ontario, on November 30th, 1969.

The late Mr. Todd was the youngest son of Mrs. James Todd, Rose Valley, P.E.I. Earl, as he was known to all, was born in Rose Valley, March 12th, 1931. Being of a kind and friendly disposition he had many friends who will regret to learn of his sudden passing. Previous to his departure to Ontario five years ago he was employed with the C.N.R. in this Province. In Hamilton, Ontario, he was employed with Findlay Fish Company Limited, where he was held in high esteem by all his co-workers.

He is survived by his wife, the former Lena Winchester, and four sons, Melvin, Jackie, Carl and David, ranging in age from seven to thirteen.

> E11. Thelma Elaine Todd, m. Arnold William Fookes, from Rhein, Saskatchewan. They live in Calgary and had issue:
> F1. Ronald Alexander Fookes.
> F2. Robert Bradley Fookes.
> F3. Catherine Faye Fookes.
> F4. Lyle William Fookes.
>
> C2. Ewen MacIntosh, 1874-1906, died in Calgary from typhoid fever, his body was taken back to the Island and buried in Highfield Cemetery, He was married to Annie Walker. They had two girls:
> D1. Rita MacIntosh, who died young.
> D2. Daughter.

A Charlottetown newspaper carried the following item:

> A wire has been received by John Walker, North River, announcing the death of his son-in-law Ewen MacIntosh, aged 32, who died from typhoid fever at Calgary on Wednesday the 10th inst. The deceased was the eldest son of Alexander MacIntosh of Stanchel and leaves to mourn a

widow and two small children and two brothers in Calgary; a father, mother, two sisters and a brother at home. The remains are expected to be brought to the Island for interment. Mr. Walker's family has been heavily afflicted recently, his son Daniel having died in Manitoba from typhoid fever about a year ago. The late Mr. MacIntosh was three years a resident of Calgary and was a carpenter by trade.

 C3. Margaret Ann MacIntosh, 1875-1963, m. James Alfred Thomas, who had been married to her sister. They lived in Boston, with issue:
  D1. Cecil Henry Thomas, 1895-1919, gassed in WWI and died soon after returning home.
  D2. Myrtle Alexandra Thomas, 1898-1953, m. Wilbur Banks. They lived in Boston, with issue:
   E1. Margaret Banks, m. Robert Heseleton.
   E2. Doris Banks, m. John Swenson.
   E3. Elva Banks, m. Arthur Sausa.
   E4. Paul Banks, married.
  D3. Elva Wellington Thomas, 1900-1966, m. Reginald Gibbs. They lived in Boston, with issue:
   E1. James Alfred Gibbs, married.
  D4. Olive Maude Thomas, m. 1) Charles Lyons. They lived in California, 2) Fred Wellington. Children with Charles Lyons were:
   E1. Doris Margaret Lyons.
   E2. James Alfred Lyons.
  D5. Rebecca Margarite Thomas, m. Jack Wilson, with issue:
   E1. John Wilson, m. Joan Boswick.
  D6. Dolina Alice Thomas, born 1906, died in infancy.
  D7. James Samuel Thomas, born 1908, died in infancy.
  D8. Jane Thomas, m. Donald Banks, nephew of

Wilbur Banks above and son of John Banks and Rebecca MacIntosh. They lived in the U.S.A. with two children:
    E1. Janice Banks.
    E2. John Banks.
    D9. Ewen Earl Thomas, m. Elizabeth _____.
C4. John Angus MacIntosh, 1878–1927, buried in Burnsland Cemetery, Calgary. He m. Christina MacPherson. They lived in Three Hills, Alberta. They had no family. When John died, Christina sold the farm in Three Hills and moved to B.C.
C5. Sarah MacIntosh, m. Frederick Elias King, Pugwash, Nova Scotia. He was killed in the battle of Paschendale, France, in the First World War. They had issue:
    D1. Celia Frances King, m. Albert Ward, Mass., U.S.A., with issue:
        E1. Lillian Frances Ward, m. Arthur Frederick Cross, Chicago. They had issue:
            F1. Susan Cross, m. 1) John Stephen Zintel, 2) Paul Williams. She died young and left no family.
            F2. Douglas Cross, m. 1) Susan Doucett, with issue:
                G1. Karen Kimberly Cross, living in Texas.
            Douglas married 2) Eveline Marie Hince, living in Birch Bay, Washington State, with issue:
                G2. Douglas Marcel Cross.
                G3. Alexandre Frederick Cross.
            F3. Bonnie Cross, m. 1) Richard Allen Santo, with issue:
                G1. Peter Jason Santo.
            Bonnie married 2) John Leonhardt Swingle,

living in San Diego, California, with issue:
    G2. Peter Jason Swingle (formally adopted by John).
    G3. Laurie Alexandra Swingle, m. Geoffrey Joseph Harms, living in Los Angeles.
F4. Michael Cross, m. Barbara Traver, living in San Diego.
F5. Earl Cross, m. Gloria Alvira Preciado. They live in Seattle, with issue:
    G1. Christina Marie Cross.
    G2. Rachel Ileana Cross.
    G3. Sylvia Frances Cross.
E2. Frederick Warner Ward, never married.
E3. Alberta Shirley Ward, m. Gary Miller, living in Los Angeles, with issue:
    F1. Paris Natalie Miller, m. Joseph Michael Haramic, living in Orange County, California, with issue:
        G1. Joseph Jon Haramic.
        G2. Nicole Renee Haramic.
    F2. Rike David Miller, m. Ivhis Jensen, living in Riverside County, California, with issue:
        G1. David Rike Miller.
D2. Frederick Elias King, Jr., m. 1) Milda Bond, with issue:
    E1. Fred King, Jr.
    E2. Brian King.
Fred married 2) Yvonne _____. They lived in Ontario, issue:
    E3. Patrick King.
    E4. Celia Lynn King.
    E5. Sharon King.
D3. Richard Alexander King, m. 1) Gladys Canmore, no issue. He m. 2) Alice Haskell, living in Ontario, with issue:

E1. Marguerite Elizabeth King.
E2. Marilyn Louise King.
He married 3) Cullen Rae Allen, with issue:
E3. Richard Earl King.
E4. Donna King.
E5. Bill King.
E6. Bob King.

D4. John Ewen King, m. Elsie _____, from England. They lived in Ontario and had issue:
E1. Diane King.
E2. Janice King.
E3. Barbara King.
E4. Carol Ann King.
E5. Michael King.
E6. Lois King.

D5. Mary Elizabeth King, m. John Tweedie. They lived in Sydney, N.S., and had issue:
E1. Hugh John Tweedie, m. Sharon Shaw, living in Cape Breton, with issue:
F1. Michele Elizabeth Tweedie.
F2. Patrick Tweedie.
F3. Craig Tweedie.
F4. Loran Tweedie.
E2. Bonnie Jean Frances Tweedie, m. 1) James McInnis, with issue:
F1. Janice McInnis.
F2. Grant McInnis.
F3. Sarah McInnis.
Bonnie m. 2) Tex Burris, living in Fredericton, N.B.
E3. Eric Lamont Tweedie, m. Lynn MacPherson, living in Pennsylvania.

C6. Richard Lee MacIntosh, 1881–1943, left P.E.I. in 1902, with his brother John and homesteaded in the Three Hills district of Alberta. In 1909, he married Laura Miller, d. 1942, who was born in Brandon, Manitoba, but moved to Alberta with her family in 1902, to a farming area east of Calgary. Richard and Laura farmed in Three Hills until 1915 when they moved to Cheadle, Alberta, and in 1926, moved to Calgary. They had issue:

D1. William Alexander MacIntosh, 1912–1998, lived in Calgary, never married.

D2. Laurie Lamont MacIntosh, m. Walter Gillingham, living in Calgary, with issue:

E1. Kenneth Gillingham, m. Anne Ervick. They lived in Edmonton, Alberta, and had issue:

F1. Laura Gillingham, m. Ryan MacMillan, Calgary.

E2. Robert Gillingham.

D3. Hazel Isabelle MacIntosh, 1916–1943, m. Fred Acorn, Calgary, Alberta, with issue. Hazel died leaving Willa at age 2 and twins, Judy and Joanne, at only 14 months, who were adopted by relatives on their father's side:

E1. Willa Acorn McGlenn, m. Michael Phillips, living in Sequim, in Washington State, with issue:

F1. Lori Phillips, married with 2 sons.

F2. Jennifer Phillips, married with 1 son.

F3. Brian Phillips, married with 4 children.

F4. Eric Phillips.

E2. Joanne Acorn McGlenn, m. Thomas Brightman, Livermore, California, with issue:

F1. Dean Brightman.

F2. Diana Brightman.

E3. Judy Acorn Glandon, twin of Joanne, m. Robert Yearout, living in Durango, Colorado, with issue:

F1. Stephanie Yearout, married with one

child.

F2. Lisa Yearout, married with one child.

C7. Donald MacIntosh, 1884-1975, m. his cousin Sarah Hume, 1889-1968. She was the daughter of John Hume and Mary Elizabeth Lamont, Wood Islands. Donald and Sarah sold their farm in Stanchel and moved to Alberta in 1917, eventually settling in Meadowview, near Barrhead, Alberta. Their children are:

D1. Eva Frances MacIntosh, 1911–1922.

D2. John Ludovick MacIntosh, 1912–1986, lived in Meadowview, Alberta, m. Ada Richmond, with issue:

E1. Shirley Patricia MacIntosh, m. Andy Meier, with issue:

F1. Lance Andrew Meier.

F2. Lori-Anne Meier.

E2. Donald William MacIntosh, m. Janice Switzer, living in Devon, Alberta, with issue:

F1. Belinda Lee MacIntosh, m. David Allan Tryhurn, with issue:

G1. Kyle Cody Tryhurn.

F2. Bonnie Lynn MacIntosh, m. Boyd Melvin Bruvold, with issue:

G1. Nicole Katherine Bruvold.

G2. Kelsey Bruvold.

E3. Ian Douglas MacIntosh, m. Sherry Weiss, with issue:

F1. Sherilyn Elizabeth MacIntosh, m. Charles Peter Rodger.

E4. Jo-Anne Alberta MacIntosh, m. Theodore Cymbaluk, Keephills, Alberta, with issue:

F1. Kevin Patrick Cymbaluk, m. Rachel Allison Kuelne, with issue:

G1. Gregg Loyd Cymbaluk.

G2. Gary Martin Cymbaluk.
G3. Jordon Kevin Cymbaluk.
G4. Amy Jo-Anne Cymbaluk.
F2. Kristen Jo-Anne Cymbaluk, m. Scott Mason, with issue:
G1. Sunni Alicia Mason.
G2. Laim Aaron Mason.
F3. Leon Martin Cymbaluk, m. Sarah Beth Elsass, with issue:
G1. Kamilla Cymbaluk.
F4. Jeffrey Theodore Cymbaluk, m. Judy Beth Ling, with issue:
G1. Caetria Karis Cymbaluk.
G2. Thadden Elis Cymbaluk.
G3. Brisa Jane Cymbaluk.
G4. Abrienne Kierra Cymbaluk.
E5. Marlene Loralie MacIntosh, m. Andrew Hrycak, from Coyote, Alberta, with issue:
F1. Anita Lynn Hrycak, m. Tony With, with issue:
G1. Jacob Bryan With.
G2. Rachael Jasmine With.
G3. Zakery Andrew With.
F2. Ivan Hrycak, has a son:
G1. Joshua Hrycak.
F3. Karen Denice Hrycak.
F4. Sarah Jean Hrycak, has a daughter:
G1. Ashlee Dawn Hrycak.
Marlene m. 2) Paul Robinson.
E6. Dale Lamont MacIntosh, m. Sharon Stevens, with issue:
F1. Merrily Joan MacIntosh, m. Tim Leskin.
F2. Holly Dale MacIntosh, m. Kurt Jones.
E7. Renaldo Vachel MacIntosh.
D3. Richard MacIntosh, 1914–1967, unmarried.

D4. William Alexander MacIntosh, 1915–1994, served in the Canadian Navy during World War II, m. Clara Archibald. They farmed in Meadowview, Alberta, with issue:
    E1. Sandra Jean MacIntosh, m. Brian Lee, living in Edmonton, with issue:
        F1. Corrina Nora Lee.
        F2. Deanna Marie Lee.
    E2. Rodney William MacIntosh, m. 1) Linda Fiest, she had two children:
        F1. Michael Fiest.
        F2. Lyndon Fiest.
    Rodney m. 2) Sharon Adzick, with issue:
        F1. Cody William MacIntosh.
        F2. Chance Travis MacIntosh.
    E3. Murray Dwayne MacIntosh, m. Tami Jane Bouchard, living in Meadowview, Alberta, with issue:
        F1. Tammy MacIntosh.
        F2. Bradley Victor MacIntosh.
        F3. Douglas Murray MacIntosh.
    E4. Glen Stuart MacIntosh, m. Erna Jensen, living in Edmonton, with issue:
        F1. Autumn Paris Jensen MacIntosh.
D5. Mary Elizabeth MacIntosh, 1917–1989, m. Jim Renfrew, Victoria, B.C., with three stepchildren:
    E1. James Robert Renfrew, m. Judith Wilma Braden, with issue:
        F1. James Renfrew.
        F2. Janelle Renfrew.
    E2. Jeanne Arlene Renfrew, m. Rick Hutchison, with issue:
        F1. Jarin Hutchison.
        F2. Joel Hutchison.
    E3. Judy Lynn Renfrew.

D6. Ewen Lamont MacIntosh, 1920–1990, wounded in France during the Second World War,. After the war he farmed in Meadowview, Alberta, m. Sylvia Horne, with issue:
  E1. Marilyn Carol MacIntosh, died at age 15.
  E2. Kathleen Joan MacIntosh, m. David Hudson, living in Red Deer, Alberta, with issue:
    F1. Alison Mary Lynn Hudson.
    F2. Devin Lamont Hudson.
    F3. Melissa Kathleen Hudson.
    F4. Sharlene Rosalie Hudson.
    F5. Elsa Suzannah Hudson.
    F6. Emily Sarah Hudson.
    F7. David Eugene Hubert Hudson.
    F8. Eloise Catherine Hudson.
    F9. Eliza Amelia Hudson.
    F10. Erin Maria Hudson.
    F11. Ellen Frances Hudson.
    F12. Eileen Jessie Hudson.
    F13. Samuel George Hudson.
    F14. Esther Isabella Hudson.
  E3. Darrell Charles MacIntosh, 1954–1980, m. Patricia Rose, with issue:
    F1. Christina Marie MacIntosh, 1978–1998.
D7. Edith Alberta MacIntosh, 1918–1919, daughter of Donald MacIntosh and Sarah Hume, died aged 6 months.
D8. Donna MacIntosh, 1921–1968, served in the Armed Services during World War Two. After the war, she m. Alan Ewart, with issue:
  E1. Daniel Ewart, m. Sharon Properzi, living in Chase, B.C., with issue:
    F1. Kimberly Laine Ewart, m. Ron Sanders.
    F2. Danielle Dawn Ewart, m. Wes Chabot, with issue:

G1. Terrahynn Chabot.
E2. Neil Ewart, m. Lynn _____, living in Chase, B.C., no family.
E3. Judy Ewart, m. Gary Agnew, living in Barrhead, Alberta,. with issue:
  F1. Leta Dona Agnew.
  F2. Kyle Agnew.
E4. Jean Ewart, m. Ted Treget, living in Edmonton, with issue:
  F1. Eric Brent Treget.
  F2. Katherine Judith Treget.
  F3. Robert Ewart Treget.
E5. Leta Ewart, m. Ken Babb, living in Brooks, Alberta, with issue:
  F1. Jamie Leroy Babb.
  F2. Alan Babb, 1977–1989, twin of Jamie, died at age twelve of asthma.
E6. Charles Ewart, living in Chase, B.C., not married.
D9. Gladys Isabel MacIntosh, 1922–1998, m. Cliff Lowry, both deceased. They lived in Sangudo, Alberta, with issue:
  E1. Mavis June Lowry, m. 1) Joseph Guretzki. They lived in Vancouver, with issue:
    F1. Corrine Melany Guretzki, m. 1) Dean Peters, 2) David McConchie, in Surrey, B.C.
    F2. Carla Guretzki, twin of Corrine, m. 1) Roy Friesen, who died in a helicopter accident, 2) Frank Imre Sipocz. Her children from Roy Friesen are:
      G1. Tiffany Alexandria Friesen.
      G2. Jessie Dale Friesen.
    F3. Tamara Charlene Guretzki, m. 1) Marvin Penner, 2) Guy Robinson, from New Zealand, now living in New Zealand, with issue:

G1. Kyasha Arrielle Robinson.

G2. Veshalla Robinson.

F4. Landon Joseph Guretzki, living in Vancouver.

E2. Dennis Raymond Lowry, living on the original homestead in Sangudo, Alberta, m. 1) Pat Miller, with issue:

F1. Shon Lowry.

Dennis married 2) Lynne Hampson, with issue:

F2. Patrick Skye Lowry.

Dennis married 3) Cheryl Samuels, from Santa Barbara, California.

E3. Iris Isabel Lowry, m. Nels Tuftin, living in Drayton Valley, Alberta, with issue:

F1. Darren Lowery Tuftin and Tracy Ross have two children:

G1. Colton Ross Tuftin.

G2. Braiden Tuftin.

F2. Dean Nelson Dennis Tuftin, living in Oregon, had a son with Nicole Kurylo:

G1. Matthew Kurylo.

Dean married Leslie Denton.

E4. Delaina Lynn Lowry, m. Ronald Rijken, living in Fox Creek, Alberta, with issue:

F1. Jordon Rijken.

F2. Christian Rijken.

F3. Rachel Rijken.

F4. Miriam Rijken.

D10. Lawrence MacIntosh, served overseas during World War Two, m. Kay Seibert, living in Red Deer, Alberta, with issue:

E1. Judy Lynn MacIntosh, m. Larry Kemshead, living in Red Deer, Alberta, with issue:

F1. Davin Edward Lawrence Kemshead.

F2. Megan Jan Kemshead.

E2. Gary Donald MacIntosh, m. Shelly Sawula, living in Red Deer, with issue:
    F1. Sean Garry MacIntosh.
    F2. Mark Donald MacIntosh.
E3. Janis Kim MacIntosh, m. Warren Bell, living in Red Deer, with issue:
    F1. William Wryley Bell.
    F2. Scott Alexander Bell.
    F3. Nicholas Bartholomew Bell, twin of Scott.
    F4. Stuart MacIntosh Bell.
D11. Reta Margaret MacIntosh, m. Tom Sandwith, from Victoria, B.C., with issue:
    E1. Joan Margaret Sandwith, m. Ken Bond, living in Black Creek, B.C., with issue:
        F1. Barbara May Bond, m. Josh Erickson.
        F2. Jeanine Catherine Bond.
    E2. William Ian Sandwith, m. Terry Shepherd, living in Victoria, B.C., with issue:
        F1. Emily Samantha Kate Sandwith.
D12. Katherine Mavis MacIntosh, m. Kenneth Sandwith, twin of Tom above. They live in Victoria, B.C., with issue:
    E1. John Robert Sandwith.
    E2. Elizabeth Rita Sandwith, m. William Gordon, living in Victoria, B.C. with issue:
        F1. Katherine Joy Gordon and Joshua Kyle Floyd, have two children:
            G1. Kyle William Floyd.
            G2. Jarid Andrew James Gordon.
    Katherine m. 2) Louis Frank Anthony Pagani.
        F2. Jubal Jeramiah Gordon.
    E3. Earl Sandwith, m. Theresa Lynn Pretty, living in Victoria, B.C., with issue:

F1. Michael Earl Sandwith.
E4. James Sandwith, m. Karla Philippson, with issue:
F1. Sara Anne Marie Sandwith.
F2. James Gerald Sandwith (Hamish).
F3. Zoe Oliva Sandwith.
E5. Kenneth Sandwith, m. Cynthia Bohnert, with issue:
F1. Jordon Thomas Sandwith.
F2. Mary Joy Sandwith.
F3. Mary Sandwith.
E6. Thomas David Sandwith, m. Heather Louise Spencer, with issue:
F1. Carly Christine Sandwith.
F2. Spencer Thomas Sandwith.
D13. Murdock MacIntosh, 1927–1999, m. 1) Lillian Hernstead, with issue:
E1. Renee, a step child.
E2. Colin MacIntosh, m. 1) Debra Adams, with issue:
F1. Renae MacIntosh.
Colin m. 2) Sandra Hayter, with issue:
F2. Emerson MacIntosh.
Murdy m. 2) Yvonne Richmond, who was a sister to his brother John's wife and the widow of Leslie Lind. She had three children from that marriage:
E1. Lois Lind.
E2. Joyce Lind, m. Ray Gabal, living in Whitecourt, Alberta.
E3. Marjory Lind, m. Don Schmaus. They farm in the Thunder Lake District, Alberta.
D14. Lillian MacIntosh, a noted author, she taught school for a number of years and is the author of, among others, *The Gentle Gamblers*, *The Tender Years* and *A Full House*, m. Reg Ross, living in

Drayton Valley, Alberta, with issue:
- E1. Kim Murdock Ross, died as a baby.
- E2. Lonnie Wayne Ross.
- E3. Erin Todd Ross, m. Pamela Penner, three step children:
    - F1. Heidi Penner.
    - F2. Cody Penner.
    - F3. Tricia Penner.

D15. David MacIntosh, m. Hilda Karp, living on the old home in Meadowview, Alberta, with issue:
- E1. Wayne David MacIntosh, m. Charlene Snider, two step children:
    - F1. Kimberly Snider.
    - F2. Jessica Snider.
- E2. Charlotte Fay MacIntosh, m. Marlow Currie, with issue:
    - F1. Adina Lynn Currie.
    - F2. Nolan Marlow Currie.
- E3. Raymond Alan MacIntosh, m. Heather Jean Bonin, with issue:
    - F1. Amanda Jean MacIntosh.
    - F2. Kayla Ruby MacIntosh.
- E4. Karen Donna MacIntosh, m. Terry Aubrey Ladan, with issue:
    - F1. Aubrey David Ladan.
    - F2. Cassidy Marie Ladan.

C8. Frances MacIntosh, died young in 1907.

C9. Rebecca MacIntosh, b. January 22, 1888, m. John Banks. They lived in Bridgetown, Nova Scotia, with issue:
- D1. Willard Banks, m. Marion _____, with issue:
    - E1. A daughter.
- D2. Donald Banks, m. Jane Thomas, daughter of Jim Thomas and Margaret Macintosh. They lived in the U.S.A. with two children:

     E1. Janice Banks.
     E2. John Banks.
  D3. Clement Banks. married with a family in the U.S.A.
  D4. Warren Banks, married and living in Maine.
  D5. Russell Banks, married and living in the U.S.A.
  D6. Minnie Alberta Banks, died aged 10 years.
  D7. Jean Banks, m. Eldon Geddes. They lived in Dartmouth, with issue:
     E1. James Geddes, m. Dianne Geddes, living in Dartmouth, N.S.
     E2. Garry Geddes.

Malcolm Lamont

B2. Malcolm Lamont, 1848-1928, son of Ewen Lamont and Sarah MacPherson, m. Jessie Gillis, died 1938, age 88, daughter of William Gillis and Christy MacLeod, Orwell Cove. Malcolm and Jessie lived in Dundee, P.E.I., where he was a wheelwright. Sir Andrew MacPhail in his book *The Master's Wife*, recounts how Malcolm had built a farm cart for his father. "Fifty four years afterwards, as appeared from the Master's books, I sent for this same man to survey the cart, as I suspected it required some repairs. He admitted that the vehicle had not lasted as long as it should, and he feared he 'must have put bad stuff in it.' He was willing to make the replacements free of charge, as he wished to maintain his reputation for sound work."

His obituary in a local newspaper states that:

… Malcolm saw Lyndale and surrounding districts, a young, struggling colony of settlers from the Highlands of Scotland still in the midst of clearing away the primeval forest. He belonged to a generation that witnessed changes, in many spheres of life, such as no age has seen through all the Christian era. Malcolm Lamont's rule of life from boyhood to the end was Micah's motto: "do justly, love mercy and walk humbly with thy God." He was one of the many trophies of grace that bore testimony to the divine power of "Old Minister MacDonald's" revivals. It is surely a unique tribute to that remarkable evangelist's memory that for nearly a century, obituaries in the public press, from time to time, continued to record that this, and that departed one, who kept the faith and died in the blessed hope, was a convert under his ministry. A very few years hence the last of those interesting converts shall have passed from the earth. Mr. Lamont occasionally wielded the rhymster's pen—once at least with considerable success, when he translated a hymn that is still sung in MacDonaldite meetings:

> *As the end of my day*
> *In this body of clay*
> *As my time of departure's near me*
> *There will pass from my tongue*
> *To the ears of the young,*
> *Timely words if you choose to hear me.*

Deceased was an eager student of scripture: and though of a retiring disposition, was always ready when challenged to contend earnestly for the faith once delivered to the saints …

Malcolm and Jessie had issue:
    C1. Christy Sarah Lamont, who died in 1987 at the age of 107 years and 4 months. She was married to Laughlin "Donald Ban" MacPherson, 1863-1951, Lyndale. They raised a family of nine, all born at home. Christy Sarah had the unique record of never having spent a night in any hospital. Their family was:
        D1. Donald MacPherson, m. Doris Dawe, from Ontario. They lived in Toronto, Ontario, and had

no family.
D2. Christine MacPherson, 1907–1994, m. Alex MacKinnon, 1892-1966, from Strathlorne, Cape Breton, but who operated a barbershop with his brother for many years in Boston, Mass. They retired to P.E.I. and had no family.
D3. Jessie MacPherson, 1909–1929, was working in Cambridge, Mass., where she died suddenly. Her body was taken home to be buried in Orwell Head. Her obituary reads:

The passing of Miss Jessie MacPherson of Kinross, at Concord Street Hospital, Cambridge, Mass., was keenly felt by all who knew and loved her. Although only in her twentieth year, she showed true appreciation for the higher and better things of life and all her acts reflected a true Christian faith and spirit of worth. Her outlook in life bore testimony to this spirit and has left its mark on the minds of many.

With rare cheerfulness, she performed her duties in the home, the community, the church, and her happy life, like a beautiful flower, radiated joy.

D4. Lamont MacPherson, m. Ruth _____. They had no family, living in B.C.
D5. Duncan MacPherson, m. Viola Gillespie, Charlottetown, with one son:
 E1. Archibald MacPherson, m. Heather Bigelow, living in Halifax with two children:
  F1. Mark MacPherson.
  F2. Ian MacPherson.
D6. Arthur MacPherson, 1914–2002, m. Jessie Lord, Tryon. They farmed in Grandview but retired to Charlottetown. Their children were:
 E1. Charles MacPherson, m. Jean MacKenzie, with issue:

   F1. Darren MacPherson.
   F2. Robert MacPherson.
  E2. Leah MacPherson, m. 1) Leo Meery, with issue:
  F1. George (Meery) Ziegler
  Leah married 2) Barry Ziegler, living in Charlottetown.
D7. Evelyn MacPherson, m. Walter Banfill, living in Mass., U.S.A., with issue:
  E1. Roger Banfill, married in the U.S.A., with two children.
  E2. Wendy Banfill, married in the U.S.A., with one child.
  E3. Douglas Banfill, not married in the U.S.A.
D8. John MacPherson, not married, living in Charlottetown.
D9. Martin MacPherson, m. Jennie Beck, Murray River. They lived in Vancouver with three children:
  E1. Geraldine MacPherson, m. James David, with five children, living in B.C.
   F1. Golda David.
   F2. Natasha David.
   F3. Tekoa David.
   F4. Jaban David.
   F5. Kea David.
  E2. Shirley MacPherson, m. Ken Saunders. They have three children in British Columbia.
   F1. Shawn Saunders.
   F2. Scott Saunders.
   F3. Rebecca Saunders.
  E3. Kimble MacPherson, m. Ferne _____ in B.C., with two children:
   F1. Lila MacPherson.
   F2. Laura MacPherson.
Martin MacPherson married 2) _____, no family.

C2. Ewen Lamont, died young.
C3. William Lamont, a twin of Ewen, died young.
C4. Mary Catherine Lamont, 1890-1975, was an R.N. and practised nursing in Chicago, Illinois, and other places before marrying Angus A.A.J. MacLeod, 1882-1967, Kinross. They farmed at Kinross and raised a family of nine:
    D1. Alexander Wesley MacLeod, 1917–1999, taught school before going overseas during WWII. His working career after the war was with the Canadian Postal Service. He is buried in Orwell Head. He married Gail Larkin, with issue:
        E1. Linda MacLeod, m. John Mullin, with issue:
            F1. Tena Mullin.
            F2. Angelina Mullin.
            F3. Abbie Mullin.
    D2. David MacLeod, 1918-1949, returning from overseas after WWII, worked in Toronto where he died from a brain tumour. He was married to Anne Bowles. They had no family.
    D3. Dorothy MacLeod ("Isabel"), m. Russell Furness, from Vernon, P.E.I., who after returning from the Second World War studied to become a veterinarian and practised in Ontario. They had issue:
        E1. Donald Furness, m. Jean Wilson, with issue:
            F1. Kathy Furness.
            F2. Jason Furness.
            F3. Lauren Furness.
        E2. David Furness, m. Anne Marie Villa, with issue:
            F1. Lee David Furness.
        E3. Sheila Furness, m. Robin Barker.
    D4. Ewen Lamont MacLeod, 1921–1992, served overseas during WWII. After the war he took over his father's farm. He never married and is buried

in Orwell Crossroads cemetery.

D5. Rhoda Maxine MacLeod, 1922-1923.

D6. Rev. John Walter MacLeod, is a minister in the Baptist church and for a time taught in their college in New Brunswick. He married Evangeline Rafuse, from Nova Scotia. They had issue:

    E1. David MacLeod.

    E2. Mark MacLeod, m. Margarete Bartelt.

    E3. Peter MacLeod, m. Tatiana Masing, with issue:

        F1. Connor Malcolm MacLeod.

        F2. Kieran Alexander MacLeod.

        F3. Jenna Elyssa MacLeod.

D7. Harold Blair MacLeod, spent his working career in the Royal Canadian Navy, m. Laura Bennett, from Seal Rocks, Newfoundland. They had issue:

    E1. Glen William MacLeod, m. Rosalyn Moore.

    E2. James MacLeod, m. Lauren Foster, with issue:

        F1. Leland James Foster MacLeod.

    E3. John Michael MacLeod.

    E4. Robert Andrew MacLeod, m. Heather _____, with issue:

        F1. Leon MacLeod.

        F2. Keillier MacLeod.

D8. Gladys MacLeod, R.N., m. George Freeze, Penobsquis, N.B. They farmed in New Brunswick and had issue:

    E1. Catherine Freeze.

    E2. David Freeze, m. Tracy _____, with issue:

        F1. Jacob George Freeze.

        F2. Hannah Catherine Freeze.

        F3. Samuel MacLeod Freeze.

        F4. John David Freeze.

D9. Mary MacLeod, m. Douglas Cameron, from Spring Hill, Nova Scotia, who was on the Police Force in Ontario. They had issue:
    E1. Wayne Cameron, m. Suzanne _____, with issue:
        F1. Martin Richard Cameron.
    E2. Linda Cameron, m. Steve Wilson, with issue:
        F1. Amanda Mary Wilson.
D10. Elinor MacLeod, Jan. 9, 1932-Feb. 8, 1932.
D11. Malcolm Kenneth MacLeod, m. Elsie Hickox. They live in Kinross, with issue:
    E1. Kenneth Martin MacLeod, m. Nancy McKenna, Iona, P.E.I. They live in Kinross, with issue:
        F1. Kaley Melissa MacLeod.
        F2. Jalen Taylor MacLeod.
    E2. Ina MacLeod ("Michelle"), m. Gerald Muller, with issue:
        F1. Kristie Melissa Muller.
        F2. Stephanie Leigh Muller.
    E3. Pamela Anne MacLeod, m. Lance Roberts, with issue:
        F1. Amelia Dawne Roberts.
        F2. Brittany Skye Roberts.
C5. John Lamont, never married. He died in Pennsylvania.
C6. Elizabeth Lamont, 1893–1980, was a widow for over fifty years. When her husband died she was left with a large family of young children. With a strong faith in her Lord and Saviour she was able to provide for them, never doubting that He who sees the sparrow fall will also supply bread for his children. She was married to David Compton, from Brooklyn, P.E.I., who died in 1930, aged 40 and was buried in

the People's Cemetery, Charlottetown. The report of his death in the local paper was as follows:

The death occurred suddenly of David Compton, C.N.R. car inspector. The deceased worked up until 1 o'clock Friday afternoon in apparently good health. He was to report for duty early Saturday morning but shortly after the trains departed word was received of his death which it is supposed was caused by heart trouble. The deceased who was forty years of age, entered the service of the C.N.R. in 1920 as car inspector, a position he held until his passing.

D1. Malcolm Henry Compton, died suddenly of a heart attack in 1936, aged 20 years. Buried in the People's Cemetery, Charlottetown.
D2. Ewen MacDougall Compton, died 1918 at 8 months, buried in Trenton, N.S.
D3. Esther Compton, 1920–1980, m. Robert Thurston, 1920–2002, Toronto, both buried in Haliburton, Ontario. Their children are:
    E1. Lila Thurston, R.N., m. Timothy Bain, living in Ballantrae, Ontario, with issue:
        F1. Brandon Bain, m. Virginia Verbal, with issue:
            G1. Kaleb Bain.
        F2. Jessica Bain.
    E2. Rodney Thurston, a building contractor, married Chantal LaRue, living in Haliburton, Ontario, with issue:
        F1. Chase Thurston.
        F2. Molly Thurston.
    E3. Irene Thurston, m. 1) Alex Ghazarossian, Ontario, 2) Mike Merritt, Ontario.
    E4. Trevor Thurston, living in Haliburton, Ont.
D4. James Wellington Compton, 1923–2002, spent

his working career with the Canadian National Railway, Toronto, where he was a supervisor in the freight department. He married 1) Lorna MacIsaac, 1923-1998, from Dunblane, P.E.I., with issue:

    E1. Ronald Compton, a financial consultant, m. Frances Stead, R.N., living in B.C., with two children:

        F1. Christopher John Compton, attending University.

        F2. Daniel James Compton.

    E2. Wendy Compton, died 1989, aged 42, was a bank manager with the Toronto Dominion Bank in Toronto, m. George Provost, of Montreal. They later moved to Oakville, Ont. Their children are:

        F1. Laurie Provost, m. David Nicholson, Oakville.

        F2. Mark Provost.

        F3. Ryan Provost.

    E3. Judy Compton, m. Roger Slawson, living in Coburg, Ontario, with one daughter.

    E4. James Compton, m. Bonnie Munro, who is descended from the Munros of Inverness Shire, Scotland, who settled in Nova Scotia. They live in Nestleton, Ontario, with issue:

        F1. Travis James Compton, attending Toronto University.

        F2. Tyler Franklin Compton.

James Wellington Compton m. 2) Olive MacNeill Silliker, O'Leary.

D5. Philip Compton, was killed in a plane crash on Tea Hill on January, 12, 1942, aged 16 years. The Charlottetown *Guardian* reported the accident:

On January 12th 1942, two aircraft based at Royal Air Force Station, Charlottetown, collided over Southport with the loss of seven lives, six airmen and one civilian, a sixteen year old youth named Compton, who presumably had received clearance for a flight in a military aircraft. He was employed by the YMCA canteen.

Both aircraft were on test flights after undergoing major maintenance. It is possible that the two aircraft were in closer proximity without being aware of each other's presence. They were outside the airport control area with no radio contact, wireless operators being unnecessary on test flights, and as there were no survivors, the board of inquiry was inconclusive.

D6. Mary Matilda Compton (Tilly), m. Harold S. MacLeod, great grandson of Ewen Lamont. Harold is the author of *The MacLeods of P.E.I.*, *The Loyalist Comptons, The Descendants of Roderick, Archibald and Catherine MacNeill* and this present volume. They live in Montague where he was one time Mayor and also Administrator of Riverview Manor. Their children are:

E1. Stephen Ross MacLeod, living in Calgary, m. 1) Barbara Lamb, with one child:

F1. Cody Stephen Francis MacLeod.

Stephen married 2) Margit Szekely, no family.

E2. Janis MacLeod, m. 1) John Roberts, she is living in Calgary, with three children:

F1. Timothy Roberts.

F2. Mathew Roberts.

F3. Amy Lynn Roberts.

Janis m. 2) Marty Samms, Calgary.

D7. Rev. David Compton, a clergyman in the Free Church of Scotland, Ontario, m. 1) Peggy Ann Morrison, Detroit. They were living in Toronto

where he was working for International Business Machines when she died suddenly at age 28. He then went back to university and to the Free Church College in Edinburgh, eventually being ordained as a minister of the Free Church. He held pastorates in The Western Charge on P.E.I., Toronto, Ontario, and Smiths Falls, Ontario. Children from this marriage are:
    E1. Philip Kevin Compton, m. Betty Geddes, living in St. Augustine, Fla., with two children:
        F1. Kevin Compton.
        F2. Heather Compton.
    E2. Catherine Compton, m. Marlo Oosterhuis, living in Clifford, Ontario, with issue:
        F1. Margaret Susan Leigh Oosterhuis.
        F2. Regan Sara Jane Oosterhuis.
David m. 2) Flora MacKenzie, Loch Carron, Scotland, a school teacher in Scotland, with the following children:
    F1. Paul Compton, school teacher in Mexico, unmarried.
    F2. Rhona Compton, m. Rowland Taylor, from England, a direct descendant of the Rowland Taylor mentioned in *Foxes Book of Martyrs*, living in Calgary, Alberta, with a son:
        G1. Luke Jonathon Taylor.
    E5. Steven Compton, m. Samantha Irons, living in Jasper, Ont. with issue:
        F1. Kayleigh Compton.
    E6. Lisa Compton, attending Queen's University.

John Lamont

B3. John Lamont, b. 1850, son of Ewen Lamont and Sarah MacPherson, was a prospector in Idaho, he is buried somewhere in the Western United States.

When still a young man, he was cutting grain with a scythe on a hot day. He sat on the cold ground to rest and cool off and it was thought that this is what caused him to take a bad attack of eczema, or perhaps modern medicine would term it psoriasis. He tried applying roofing tar on his skin, an old home remedy, with indifferent results.

In 1883, he sent a letter to his father, containing a gold nugget.

Angus Lamont

B4. Angus Lamont, 1852-1926, son of Ewen Lamont and Sarah MacPherson, m. Catherine Elizabeth MacPherson, b. 1858, from Glen William.

Angus was a school teacher and farmer. His father had given him a deed to fifty acres from the back of his farm and on this, together with the purchase of an adjoining fifty acres, he built a homestead.

When his brother Murdock sold the original Lamont homestead and moved to Stanchel, where their sister Frances was living, Angus also sold his farm and moved to that area. In 1901 he moved to Sydney, Nova Scotia.

The Sydney *Post* reports:

> Angus Lamont was a well known and respected resident of Ward V ... a public spirited citizen who took an interest in all movements for community betterment.
>
> He was an Elder in the Presbyterian Church and Superintendent in one of its Sunday Schools. Mr. Lamont, who was born in Lyndale, Prince Edward Island, was a son of

Ewen Lamont, a leading Elder under Rev. Donald MacDonald, a minister of provincial renown in his day.

Mr. Angus Lamont was a public school teacher for about 20 years.

Latterly for some time he carried on farming in Stanchel and in 1901 he removed to Sydney, Cape Breton, where he

Angus Lamont's grocery store in Sydney

successfully carried on a grocery business. It is a remarkable fact that although the trouble from which he died was an inward cancer, yet he suffered almost no pain. Until the day he entered the hospital he went cheerfully about his work as usual, and after the operation passed peacefully into his rest.

Mr. Lamont was from his youth intensely religious and to the last kept abreast of all ecclesiastical movements and doctrinal developments. He contended all his life for the faith once given to the saints. He was an elder in St. James Church, Sydney, till that church entered Union, when he quietly but firmly severed from its communion—declaring his belief that in this creed-dissolving age it was the duty of Christians to hold forth an unwavering testimony on the essentials of the faith. This he professed to find in the continuing Presbyterian Church.

Angus Lamont is buried in Eastmount Cemetery, Witney Pier, Cape Breton. His wife's name is not on the marker.

Angus Lamont and Catherine MacPherson's children were:
C1. Sarah Lamont, b. May 18, 1881, m. Aubrey Dodson, Sydney, N.S. They had issue:
D1. Wilbur Dodson, m. Maude Head. They live in Sydney, N.S., with issue:
E1. Catherine Elizabeth Dodson, m. David Krawchuk, living in Sydney, N.S., with issue:
F1. Catherine Elizabeth Krawchuk (Cathy), m. Keith Donaldson. They have two children.
G1. Sarah Donaldson.
G2. Keith Donaldson.
E2. William Dodson, m. Margaret MacDougall, from Sunny Brae, Pictou County, Nova Scotia. They are both pharmacists with a drug store in the town of Pictou. Their children are:
F1. Bruce Dodson, attending University.
F2. Alan Dodson, attending University.
F3. Kevin Dodson, living in Ottawa.
F4. Anne Elizabeth Dodson.
E3. Sharon Dodson, m. Alfred LeDrew. They live in Sydney, and have two girls:
F1. Laura Louise LeDrew, m. Carl Phillipo, living in Bonnyville, Alberta, with issue:
G1. Grace Phillipo.
G2. Emily Phillipo.
F2. Gina Lynn LeDrew.
D2. Orlar Aubrey Dodson, served overseas in the armed forces during the Second World War. He married Louise Holly from Vancouver who also was a war veteran. They lived in Toronto, with two children:

E1. David Dodson.

E2. Doreen Dodson.

D3. William Dodson, an engineer in the U.S.A., married.

C2. Margaret Lamont, R.N., b. January 10, 1883, m. Ernest MacLeod. They lived in New York, had no family.

C3. Ann Lamont, b. January 3, 1884.

C4. Angus Lamont, b. February 8, 1885, m. Carrie from North Sydney. They had one daughter:

D1. Catherine Lamont, married in New York, with two daughters.

C5. Mary Elizabeth Lamont, b. 1887.

C6. Frances Margaret Lamont, R.N., b. 1888, m. Fredericks. They lived in New York, and had one daughter.

C7. Ewen Lamont, b. May 15, 1889.

C8. Margaret Catherine Lamont, b. 1891, m. George David Draper Martell, b. 1887, Sydney, N.S. They live in Louisburg, N.S., and had issue:

D1. Margaret Martell.

D2. Roy Ewen Martell, never married.

D3. Muriel Elizabeth Martell.

D4. Phyllis Marie Martell.

D5. Lamont Martell.

C9. John Lamont, 1893–1975, m. Effie MacIntosh, 1915–1996, daughter of Daniel and Agnes MacIntosh, from Sydney, N.S. John and Effie lived in Sydney and had two children:

D1. Angus Lamont, m. Norma Marshall, living in Miramichi, with three children:

E1. Christopher John Lamont.

E2. Jason Ewen Lamont.

E3. Jonathon Craig Lamont.

D2. John Ernest MacLeod Lamont, m. Elissa Corsano, from Sydney. They are living in Lower

Sackville, Nova Scotia, with a son:
E1. John Ryan Lamont.

At least two of Angus and Catherine's children died in childhood and are buried at Orwell Head, P.E.I.

Sarah Lamont

B5. Sarah Lamont, 1854-1915, daughter of Ewen Lamont and Sarah MacPherson, m. Donald Gillis, 1841-1926. They lived in Orwell. Her obituary, which appeared in a local newspaper, states that:

In early life she was brought to a knowledge of God and her Saviour in the washing of regeneration and renewing of the Holy Spirit, and throughout her life both in the home and community she manifested a consistent Christian character and disposition which endeared her to family and friends. During her illness she was sustained by the Hope of Glory which shed great comfort upon those who were with her. She leaves a sorrowing husband, two sons and four daughters, all of whom, except one son who is in British Columbia, were near her during her illness. The family and friends felt keenly the loss of one who was so faithful as wife, mother and friend.

Sarah and Donald's children were:
C1. Catherine Anne Gillis (Katie), 1878–1963, m. Donald John MacLeod (locally known as Jack John Neil), 1875–1955. They farmed in Orwell, later moved to Uigg. They had no family.
C2. John Alexander Gillis, b. Dec 14, 1880 m. Lillan Grace Rona Cooper. They lived in British Columbia, with issue:
D1. George Warren Gillis.

D2. Sarah Gillis, married George Alexander Smith with children;
  E1. Karen Smith m. Maurice Linneberg, living in B.C. They have a son:
    F1. Cody Maurice Alexander Linneberg.
  D3. Mary Gillis.
  D4. Margaret Gillis.
C3. Sarah Gillis, 1883–1962, m. John Findlay MacDonald, 1871–1917, Kinross, with issue:
  D1. Donald John MacDonald, 1913–1927.
  D2. Peter MacDonald, of San Francisco, m. Helen Polapeck. They lived in California
  D3. Sally MacDonald, graduated from the P.E.I. School of Nursing in 1938, m. _____ Hurdle. They lived in Niagara Falls, Ontario, and had issue:
    E1. Sheila Hurdle, m. David Gohm, living in Niagara Falls. They have a family.
C4. Mary Rachel Gillis, 1885–1961, m. Alexander Gillis, 1882–1964. They lived in Head of Montague, with issue:
  D1. Sadie Gillis, 1914–1934, m. Gordon Ross, a miller at Vernon River, no issue.
  D2. Donald Gillis, m. Bobby Ross, sister of Harvey of Lower Montague. They lived in Charlottetown, with issue:
    E1. Ross Gillis, m. Eileen Hayter, of High Bank. They live in Charlottetown, with issue:
      F1. Dwayne Gillis.
      F2. Grant Gillis.
    E2. Donna Gillis, m. Eddie Cudmore, living in Charlottetown, with issue:
      F1. Donald Cudmore.
      F2. Kevin Cudmore.
      F3. Karen Cudmore, m. Greg MacIsaac, with issue:

G1. Alexander MacIsaac.
D3. Archie Gillis, m. Ann Cameron, of Charlottetown. They live in Pictou, Nova Scotia, issue:
   E1. Dorothy Gillis, R.N., m. Jim McConnell, Scotsburn, N.S. Jim operates the Scotsburn Creamery. They have four daughters:
      F1. Dianne McConnell, m. Arnold Cameron, with issue:
         G1. Katelyn Cameron.
         G2. Samuel Cameron.
      F2. Kim McConnell, m. Gregory Duncan, with issue:
         G1. Hannah Duncan.
         G2. _____.
      F3. Nancy McConnell, m. Charles Manner.
      F4. Susan McConnell, graduate of Dalhousie University.
   E2. Gordon Gillis, graduated from Dalhousie law school, and is Deputy Minister of Justice with the Nova Scotia Government. He m. Rosie Price, from Louisburg, living in Dartmouth with a family.
      F1. Gordon James Gillis.
D4. John Gillis, 1918–1991, taught school before going overseas in WWII. After the war he worked in Montreal, where he met and married Kay MacPherson, Malcolm "George's" daughter from Belfast. They lived in Montreal and had four daughters:
   E1. Glenda Gillis, m. Stephen Essam. They live in Stouffville, Ontario, with issue:
      F1. Richard James Llewellyn Essam.
   E2. Ann Louise Gillis, living in Montreal.
   E3. Elizabeth Joyce Gillis, m. George Kourakos. They live in Roxboro, near Montreal, with issue:

F1. Julie Ann Kourakos.
F2. Jonathon Matthew Malcolm Kourakos.
E4. Joan Marion Gillis, living in Montreal.
D5. William Gillis, 1919–1957, was also a WWII veteran. After the war he married Isabel Shaw, from Uigg. They lived in B.C., where he was killed in a road accident leaving three daughters and a son. His obituary in a Charlottetown newspaper reads:

In the midst of life we are in death. These words were never more applicably spoken than when word was received that William Gillis had been instantly killed as the result of a car accident which occurred at Nanaimo, B.C., on New Year's Eve.

Billy, as he was familiarly known, was well liked and highly esteemed by all who knew him, a good neighbour and a friend always willing to lend a helping hand to those in need as was true on the night of the fatality. He had just stepped out of the car to help another who was stranded when a third car happened along and due to the icy conditions was unable to avoid striking the bystanders thus causing two fatalities.

He was posted to the Middle East, during WWII, where he served until the end of the war. He then purchased a farm at Victoria Cross where he resided until one year ago when he and his family moved to Nanaimo, B.C. ...

The children of William Gillis and Isabel Shaw are:
E1. Carol Gillis, living on the Pacific Coast, m. 1) _____, with issue:
F1. Monique Candace Horvath, m. Brendan Canavan, both teaching in Japan.
F2. Stephen John Horvath, not married, a fisherman on the Pacific Coast.

Carol m. 2) Ronald Hungle.

E2. David Gordon Gillis, is a partner of Janice Adams, no family.

E3. Elizabeth Ann Gillis (Betty), m. 1) _____ Smesney, with issue:

    F1. Rudy Quentin Smesney, died at age 19 in April 1997 after being hit by a car as he was running across the highway.

    F2. Tara Isabelle Smesney, attending university.

Betty married 2) Jeff Armstrong, living in B.C.

E4. Pamela Margaret Gillis, m. Raymond Telford. They live in B.C., with issue:

    F1. Selby Telford m. Tamara _____, with issue:

        G1. Taylor Telford.

        G2. Ryan Telford.

    F2. Natasha Telford, m. Clint Walsh, with issue:

        G1. Christopher Walsh.

D6. David Roy Gillis, 1915–1983, m. Ann MacLeod, from Glen William. She was a school teacher, and he worked for MacLeod and Greene, a farm machinery agency in Montague. They lived in Montague, and had no family.

D7. Gordon Gillis, 1922–1946, was severely wounded in Italy during WWII and died soon after returning to P.E.I.

C5. Ewen Lamont Gillis, 1887–1975, m. Lillian Stewart, 1896–1956, of Belle River. They farmed in Orwell, where she was killed by a truck when she was crossing the road to the mailbox. The local paper reported:

Tragedy again struck close to homes and hearts in this vicinity when a second fatality in a little over a month occurred in Orwell, this time claiming the life of Mrs. Ewen Gillis on December 1st.

As already stated in the press, the accident took place when the late Mrs. Gillis went to the road for the mail—a daily errand in which she took delight, as she had many thoughtful relatives from outside who regularly remembered her by letter or gift. Also it was her custom when returning home to visit with her elderly friend and neighbour, Mrs. John Martin.

The late Mrs. Gillis was predeceased by her son John, who died several years ago in his early twenties and also by several children who died in infancy.

> D1. John D. Gillis, 1918–1942, died suddenly as a young man. A local paper carried the following:

The community of Orwell was shocked to learn of the sudden passing away on March 3rd of John D. Gillis in the twenty-fifth year of his age. John Gillis, as he was familiarly known throughout Orwell and surrounding districts, was a very fine type of young man. He was a fine upstanding man physically and morally. He was popular with everyone and was a regular attendant of St. Andrew's United Church. He was interested in the Young People's work and was an officer of the local society. He had taken preliminary training and was awaiting his call for further service. It came a few days after he had answered the higher call. His passing is a great loss to the community where he gave promise of being a useful citizen. The loss to his parents is almost overwhelming.

> Ewen married 2) Mrs. Emily (Martin) Jenkins, no family.
> C6. Margaret Gillis, b. May 6, 1892.
> C7. Elizabeth Gillis, b. Nov 29, 1896, m. Richard

Reeves of Los Angeles.

Rebecca Lamont

B6. Rebecca Lamont, 1856–1943, was a studious, well read person. Her Bible was her constant companion and she could, and often did, hold her own with many a theologian. According to her own account she was "set free" in DeSable Church at about twelve years of age when she experienced the joy of knowing that her sins were forgiven. She danced in front of the elders' rail with all her might and main, like King David, who when an old man yet danced before the ark as it was brought back to Jerusalem (II Samuel 6:16). On her last day on earth, as her family gathered around her bed, she said "He has set before me an open door which no man can shut" (Rev. 3:8.).

She married Murdock MacNeill, 1847–1939, Little Sands, whose mother was Sarah Currie, a sister of Rebecca's grandmother. As a young man Murdock worked at building the main line of the Colonial Railroad to Upper Canada, through northern New Brunswick. He had his own horse and cart on the job and in later years used to sing several verses of a song the workers used to sing, the last line of each verse was:

How can a man support a wife on ninety cents a day?

Rebecca and Murdock had the following children:
> C1. Archie Silas MacNeill, 1881-1963, spent his working career as a carpenter in the U.S.A., During WWII he was working in the shipyards in Massachusetts and was given an award for an invention that was valuable towards the war effort. He retired from the shipyards three times, but was called back to work on two occasions, finally retiring when over seventy years of age.

He returned to P.E.I. He is buried in Little Sands and was never married.
C2. Sarah MacNeill, 1879-1900, never married.
C3. Margaret MacNeill, 1884–1990. Her obituary in a local paper reads:

... In 1901 at the age of seventeen she left for Boston, Massachusetts, her father driving her to Brush Wharf with a horse and buggy, to take the ferry to Charlottetown. The Murray Harbour Railroad was not completed at that time.

Margaret MacNeill in 1902 (seated left, front row)
Back row (left to right): Margaret and John Walter MacLeod; Sadie (Gillis) McDonald of Orwell Cove.
Front row: Margaret MacNeill; John and Mary Gillis (seated in front) of Orwell Cove; Mary K. and Alec Gillis of Lyndale

Gaelic was her first language as well as English since many of her near relatives had a limited knowledge of the English Language, having emigrated from the Island of Colonsay in 1832.

In Massachusetts she went back to school to upgrade her education in order to enrol in the Tewksbury Hospital School of Nursing, from which she graduated as a Registered

Nurse. She worked at her profession in that area until 1914, when she returned to P.E.I. to marry Roderick C. MacLeod.

They farmed in Lyndale where they raised seven children. All five of her sons were on active service during World War II.

One son, Ewen was killed in the battle of Caen, France, in 1944.

Through the years she made use of her nursing skills by acting as midwife and she assisted in a number of maternity cases in that area.

During World War II, due to a shortage of nurses, she practised her profession in the Montague Hospital and in the P.E.I. Hospital. After the war she operated a nursing home which she continued until well into her nineties. She was active almost to the last and retained her faculties to the end.

Early in life she put her trust in Christ as her Saviour and throughout a long life she never doubted the goodness and mercy of her Lord. During the last few weeks, although she endured intense pain, on one occasion when her son and his wife visited her, she requested they sing the 34th Psalm, beginning with the verse:

> *O taste and see that God is good,*
> *Who trusts in Him is blest,*
> *Fear God His saints, none that Him fear,*
> *Shall be with want oppressed.*

To pass from this life, to her, was not an end but rather a beginning for she "looked for a city whose builder and ruler is God." In her own words, she was going home.

She leaves to mourn her passing her sons: Reg in Halifax, N.S., Wendell in Brudenell, P.E.I., Hector in B.C., Harold in Montague, and a daughter, Marion Leafe in Ontario. Also thirty grandchildren, forty-eight great–grandchildren, and three great-great grandchildren. A daughter Ella (Mrs.

Edison Taylor) and a son Ewen predeceased.

The funeral was held from the MacLean Funeral Home, October 20, with Rev. William Underhay officiating. Pallbearers were Roderick Taylor, Ernest MacLeod, Roderick MacLeod, Dr. Roy Campbell, Roger Gillis, and Lloyd MacDonald. Flower bearers were her granddaughter Mary Leafe and great-granddaughters Melanie Darrach, Jodi MacDonald, Ava Campion, and Chantelle Taylor. Burial was in Orwell Head Cemetery beside her husband who died in 1956.

Margaret died Oct. 17, 1990, age 106 years and two days.

Her husband, Roderick Charles MacLeod, 1877-1956, from Lyndale, was son of Charles MacLeod and Rachel MacDonald.

He was baptized and given the name of Roderick Alexander, but there were several Roderick MacLeods in the area so he became known as Roddie Charlie. When he became an adult he accepted the name Charles as his middle name and signed all documents and official papers with Roderick Charles MacLeod.

They lived in Lyndale where he was active in every community effort. He served on the Provincial Welfare Board, and was for many years an elder of the church. He was a Justice of the Peace, served as Master of Lion L.O.L., was Secretary Treasurer of the Lyndale School District, also Secretary Treasurer of the Orwell Head Church for a number of years and was chairman of the Grandview North polling division for over 50 years.

The Editor of *The Patriot*, a Charlottetown newspaper, commented:

> The funeral of Roderick C. MacLeod took place Sunday. Orwell and the district will certainly miss this fine man, always jolly, a big powerful man and one of the staunch Liberals of the district and a sound thinking man. We will all miss him. There will never be another Roddie Charlie

MacLeod, as we always knew him, and a great friend of the Patriots.

His obituary in the local paper states that:

> Orwell Head Church lost a layman in the passing of Roderick Charles MacLeod, who served faithfully as senior Elder in this congregation for upwards of forty years. Mr. MacLeod passed away at his home in Kinross on June 8th, 1956, following two months illness and three major operations, during which time he was patient in the Prince Edward Island Hospital.
>
> Born at Lyndale, P.E.I., June 3rd, 1877, where he spent the greater part of his life as a farmer, retiring to the village of Kinross three years ago. He worked actively in support of the Liberal Party since the days of Laurier. He was especially well informed in family trees, folklore and the history of his native Belfast district. He was also a member of the Orange Order. At the time of his death Mr. MacLeod was in his 80th year. Despite his advanced years he never became relegated to the chimney corner, but mind and memory remained active until the end. He never forgot a name nor a face and hospitality was for him a delight rather than a duty.

Their children were:

D1. Ella MacLeod, 1915–1957, m. Edison Taylor, 1915–1998, Millview, a descendant of the Taylors who came from Kintyre, Scotland, and settled in Wood Islands. Ella and Edison lived in Lyndale, where she died at a comparatively young age leaving a large family of girls and boys. Her obituary in the local paper states:

> Friends relatives and acquaintances were shocked and saddened to learn of the sudden and unexpected passing of

Mrs. Edison Taylor which occurred at her home in Lyndale, P.E.I. on the morning of December 4th, 1957. Mrs. Taylor, the former Ellen Elizabeth MacLeod, was the daughter of the late R.C. MacLeod and Mrs. MacLeod of Kinross. She was 42 years of age. A life though short, yet marked the end of unselfish and untiring service to home, community and God. She was a loyal member, supporter and choir member of Orwell Head United Church which suffered a distinct loss in her passing. Mrs. Taylor, who was a graduate of Prince of Wales College, taught school for a number of years. On Saturday, December 8th, funeral service was held in Orwell Head Church, conducted by her pastor, Rev. F. MacKinnon, who took as his text, Psalm 127:2: "He giveth His beloved sleep." The church could not contain the large congregation that assembled as people from far and near came to pay their respects to a friend and loved one.

Mrs. Taylor is survived by nine children ranging in age from four months to seventeen years.

> The children of Ella MacLeod and Edison Taylor are:
> E1. Margaret Leah Taylor, m. Dennis Ernest Campion from Birmingham, England. They live in Lyndale, with issue:
> F1. Julie Margaret Campion, m. Robert Bruce Blackett, Georgetown. They have two children:
> G1. Robert Aaron Blackett.
> G2. Valen Rose Blackett.
> F2. Dennis Andrew Campion, carpenter and cabinet maker, living in Lyndale, not married.
> F3. Ava Joan Campion, m. 1) James Robinson, from Pugwash, Nova Scotia, with issue:
> G1. Kassy Marie Robinson.

Ava married 2) Gordon Carter. They live near Amherst, Nova Scotia.

F4. Murray Taylor Campion, m. Elizabeth MacLean, Brudenell. They live in Lyndale.

F5. David Mark Campion, m. Shanea Bauer, from Kamloops, British Columbia. He is a Nursing Attendant in Charlottetown. They live in Mount Vernon, P.E.I., with issue:

    G1. Hannah Lynn Campion.
    G2. Rachel Mae Campion.
    G3. Sarah Anne Campion.
    G4. David Alexander Campion.

E2. Marion Taylor, m. 1) William Ross, Eldon, P.E.I. They lived in Toronto, Ont., with issue:

    F1. Kent William Ross, living in the Toronto area.
    F2. Joel Allan Ross, living in the Toronto area.

Marion married 2) George Grant. They live near Haliburton, Ontario.

E3. Prudence Elizabeth Taylor, m. Mark MacDonald, from Country Harbour Crossroads, N.S., and Mass. His mother was Isabel MacGillivary from the Cardigan area. They live in Mass., and have issue:

    F1. Michelle Lee MacDonald, m. Michael Keefe, with issue:
        G1. Spencer Campbell Keefe.
        G2. Austin Keefe.
    F2. Kimberly MacDonald, m. John Abruzzo. Their children are:
        G1. John Mark Abruzzo.
        G2. Anthony Abruzzo.
        G3. Eric Cameron Abruzzo.
    F3. Stacy Ellen MacDonald, m. Randy

Deeran.
    G1. Alexandrea Elizabeth Deeran.
E4. William Edison Taylor, m. Shirley Penny, from Ontario. They live in Ontario, with issue:
    F1. Ronald William Edison Taylor.
    F2. Michael D.J. Taylor, m. Kelly Masters, with issue:
        G1. Rebekah Marie Anne Taylor.
    F3. Louise Elizabeth Taylor, died at birth.
    F4. Brian James F. Taylor.
E5. Roderick Taylor, a businessman in Charlottetown, m. Elizabeth Keenan, R.N., from Hamilton, Ont. They live in Bethel, P.E.I. Their children are:
    F1. Chantelle Ellen Elizabeth Taylor, married Darren Wood, Mt. Herbert. They live in Guelph where he teaches in a veterinary school. They have issue:
        G1. Gavin Robert Wood.
        G2. Elijah Roderick Wood.
    F2. Matthew Taylor, living in Charlottetown.
    F3. Daniel Taylor, m. Teddi Kim Bengert. They live near Moose Jaw, Saskatchewan.
E6. Elsa Merle Taylor, died from a brain tumour June 5, 1991, aged 42 years.
E7. Samuel Judson Taylor, m. Sandra Oldfield, living in Ontario, with issue:
    F1. Shawn Gordon Taylor.
    F2. Samantha Nicolle Taylor.
E8. Harold Collings Taylor, married Wendy Knowsley, living in Ontario, with issue:
    F1. Amber Ellen Irene Taylor.
    F2. Aaron Joseph Taylor.
E9. Wendell Brian Taylor, a Charlottetown businessman, married 1) Pauline DesRoche, with

issue:
    F1. Christopher Ryan Taylor.
Wendell m. 2) Elizabeth Bagnall, Charlottetown.
    F2. Mezena Bagnall, stepdaughter.
D2. Charles Reginald MacLeod, served in the Canadian Navy during World War Two, m. Hazel MacKinnon, from Kilmuir, daughter of Carl MacKinnon. They live in Halifax, where he was a building contractor. They had issue:
    E1. Margaret Anne MacLeod, R.N., m. John Westlie, Ph.D., living in Meadowbank, P.E.I., where he is retired from teaching in the University and she is the author of historical novels set in 19th century P.E.I. They have no family.
    E2. Florence MacLeod, married Harley Harper. They both taught school in Charlottetown and live on Tea Hill, near Charlottetown, with issue:
        F1. Jonathan Harper.
        F2. Adam Harper.
    E3. Roderick MacKinnon MacLeod, m. Jean MacLellan from Noel Shore, N.S., sister of Ann MacLellan who was one time Minister of Justice in Ottawa, representing a seat in Edmonton, Alberta. Roderick and Jean are living near Halifax, with issue:
        F1. Janet Rebecca MacLeod.
        F2. Ian MacLeod.
D3. Wendell Murdock MacLeod, 1918-1997, served in the Royal Canadian Air Force during World War Two, m. Jessie MacBeth. They lived in Kinross, with issue:
    E1. Ernest MacLeod, m. Alfreda Bears, daughter of the singer John Bears. They live in Kinross, with issue:

F1. Darren MacLeod, m. Joni Garnhum, living in Kinross, with issue:
    G1. Jessica MacLeod.
F2. Darrell MacLeod, a twin, not living.

E2. Mary MacLeod, m. Neil MacDonald, Brudenell, P.E.I., with three children:
    F1. Jody MacDonald.
    F2. Dannie MacDonald.
    F3. Kimberly MacDonald.

E3. Anne MacLeod, m. 1) Aubrey Darrach, New Dominion, P.E.I., with issue:
    F1. Melanie Darrach, m. Reuben Creed, living in Lower Montague, P.E.I., with issue:
        G1. Caleb Creed.
    F2. Christopher Darrach, m. Marilyn Lewis, living in Moncton, with issue:
        G1. Canaan Darrach.
        G2. Hunter Darrach.

Anne m. 2) Donald MacLeod, Montague, with issue:
    F3. Amanda MacLeod.

E4. Ewen MacLeod, m. Anna Murnaghan, R.N., Fort Augustus. They live near Charlottetown, where he is an Insurance Estimator and Anne is a nurse at the Queen Elizabeth Hospital. They have issue:
    F1. Christa MacLeod.
    F2. Ryan MacLeod.
    F3. Shannon MacLeod.

D4. Rev. Hector MacLeod, served his country in the Armed Forces during WWII. When he returned from overseas, he took up residence in British Columbia, where he was employed with the British Columbia Department of Highways, eventually becoming Resident Engineer, having under his jurisdiction Vancouver and other smaller islands situated on the Pacific coast.

During the course of his working career he took time off work to attend and graduate from the Pambrun Bible College in Saskatchewan. Thereafter, until nearing the customary retirement age, he retained his position with the B.C. Government as well as pastoring in churches and communities, wherever he felt there was a need.

He is the author several books: *Behold the Lamb*, also *Israel, God's Timeclock*, and *Forever Forgiven*.

He married Lily Belsen, in London, England, during the war. Together they raised ten children, all living on Vancouver Island with the exception of their son Paul who lives on the mainland:

E1. Joan Miriam MacLeod, m. Rueben Ernest Jasper, with issue:
    F1. Shelly Joan Leeanne Jasper, married Brian Richard Kuhn, with issue:
        G1. Justin Richard Kuhn.
        G2. Jesse Michael Kuhn.
        G3. Tyler Matthew Kuhn.
    F2. Angela Dawn Jasper, m. Guy Robert Belanger, with issue:
        G1. Brooke Aimee Belanger.
        G2. Sara Eva Belanger.
        G3. Joshua Guy Belanger.
    F3. Kenneth Reuben Jasper, m. Michelle Stella Greenwell, with issue:
        G1. MacKenzie Cheyenne Jasper.
    F4. Michael Scott Jasper.
E2. Judith Margaret MacLeod, m. Donald George Willett, with issue:
    F1. Wendy Margaret Willett, m. Steven

Staynor.
    G1. Amanda Faye Staynor.
    F2. Timothy Eifion Willett, m. Kim Lori Ellingson, with issue:
    G1. Brendan Timothy Willett.
E3. Paul Roderick MacLeod, m. Margaret May Vickers, with issue:
    F1. Jonathan Paul MacLeod, m. Shannon Marie Chartier, with issue:
    G1. Kayla Marie MacLeod.
    G2. Carley Anne MacLeod.
    F2. Linda Margaret MacLeod, m. Darren John Olsen.
    G1. Jakob Darren Olsen.
    G2. Megan May Lanette Olsen.
    G3. Jenna Lynn Olsen.
    F3. Andrea May MacLeod, m. Douglas John Froese, with issue:
    G1. Matthew MacLeod Froese.
    G2. Mya Nicole Froese.
E4. Wendy Lynn MacLeod, m. Robert David Graham, with issue:
    F1. Dena Lynn Graham, m. James Peter Perfect, with issue:
    G1. Kendra Lynn Perfect.
    F2. Keith David Graham, m. Tamara Bernice Pellett, with issue:
    G1. Tyler David Graham.
    G2. Chelsea Michelle Graham.
    G3. Kaleb Matthew Graham.
    G4. Tiffany Leanne Graham.
E5. Matthew Barnet MacLeod, m. Candice Jean Bates, with issue:
    F1. Jolynn Ashlee MacLeod.
    F2. Janna Lee MacLeod.

E6. Daniel Peter MacLeod, m. Bonnie Lee Gale, with issue:
- F1. Lisa Beverly MacLeod.
- F2. Brittany Laurel MacLeod.
- F3. Rachelle Nicole MacLeod.

E7. Roderick Charles MacLeod, m. Noreen Joyce Miller, with issue:
- F1. Rebecca Lynn MacLeod.
- F2. Curtis Roderick MacLeod.
- F3. Luke Anthony MacLeod.
- F4. Arianne Elizabeth MacLeod.
- F5. David Cartwright MacLeod.
- F6. Andrew Hector MacLeod.

E8. Timothy Roger MacLeod, m. 1) Bonnie O'Dresgal, 2) Lorelle Jamieson, with issue:
- F1. Amelia Danielle MacLeod.
- F2. Samuel Jamieson MacLeod.

E9. Jennifer Joy MacLeod, m. Daryl Thomas Clark, with issue:
- F1. Arnold Thomas Clark.
- F2. Ashley Lyn Clark.
- F3. Kimberly Ann Clark.

E10. Dean Thomas MacLeod, unmarried.

D5. Marion Rachel MacLeod, taught school and was at one time private secretary to the Honourable J. Lester Douglas, who represented Queens County in the Federal Government in Ottawa. She married Ian S. Leafe, Birmingham, England. They live in Willowdale, Ontario, with issue:

E1. Francesca Leafe, a graduate from the Royal Conservatory of Music. She teaches music in Toronto. She married William Wright. They live near Musselman's Lake, Ontario, with issue:
- F1. Emily Wright.
- F2. Nicholas Wright.

E2. Mary Leafe, m. Calvin Weeks. They live in Stouffville, Ontario, with issue:
   F1. Carson Varey Weeks.
D6. Ewen Angus MacLeod, was killed in the Battle of Caen, France in WWII.
D7. Harold S. MacLeod, m. Mary Matilda Compton (Tilly). For a more detailed biography, see page 98, above. Their children are:
   E1. Stephen Ross MacLeod, m. 1) Barbara Lamb, Calgary, with issue:
      F1. Cody Stephen Francis MacLeod.
   Stephen m. 2) Margit Szekely, living in Calgary.
   E2. Janis Lynn MacLeod, m. 1) John Roberts, with issue:
      F1. Timothy Roberts.
      F2. Mathew Roberts.
      F3. Amy Lynn Roberts.
   Janis m. 2) Marty Samms. They live in Calgary.
C4. Mary MacNeill, 1888-1917, never married.
C5. Hugh MacNeill, 1889-1977, worked for a number of years as a conductor on the Boston street cars. When his parents became old they sent for him to come home to take over the farm in 1917. He never married.
C6. Ella MacNeill, 1891-1928, never married. On the night of her death, her father had a dream that Ella went out on the veranda of their house, which was bordered on one side by a number of fruit trees. In his dream the trees were all pure gold. In the morning, word was brought that Ella, who was being cared for by her sister Margaret in Lyndale, some twenty miles away, had died that night.

Her obituary which appeared in a local paper, reads:

At Lyndale, P.E.I., on November 10th, 1928, there passed

to her eternal reward Miss Ella MacNeill, aged 37 years and six months. She had been a patient suffering for twenty three years having developed spinal trouble at the early age of fourteen years and although everything possible was done for her, she remained an invalid.

Her death will be keenly felt by her many friends and relatives in this Province and elsewhere. Correspondence was one of her great delights and by it she entered many homes and hearts with messages of cheer, comfort and Christian joy. She also composed poems of some merit, one of which appears elsewhere. It can truly be said of her that she set her affection on things above and radiated to those about her the light of God's glory that shone within her heart.

The funeral was large. The service was conducted by her pastor, Rev. Ewen MacDougall, who spoke with feeling of the happy Christian influence Ella had on all with whom she came in contact and while he thus spoke of her, he exhorted those present to give the glory and praise to God who in Christ had wrought such blessedness within the soul of their beloved friend.

The following is one of a great number of poems written by her during her short life:

Eternity

Christ is my hope, my endless home,
Let change or desolation come,
Let the loved spot which saw my birth
Be burnt and pass with Heaven and earth,
Yet Christ remains a home for me
My portion through eternity.

Christ is my home, oh! world so gay
Invite me not with you to stay,

Ask me not of thy joys to taste
Nor on thy pleasures time to waste.
Christ is my home, to Him I flee,
My portion thro' eternity.

Christ is my home, some day I know
He'll call me hence, I'll gladly go
To dwell with him in regions bright,
Where Christ in glory waits for me,
My portion of eternity.

Christ is my home, my endless rest,
Oh! may I once lean on his breast,
Oh! happy hour when from this clay
My soul is free to fly away
To Christ, whose blood has cleansed me,
My portion thro' eternity.

C4. Edith MacNeill, 1897-2003, m. John Campbell. He was overseas in the Armed Services during the First World War. When he returned from Europe he worked on the Canadian Prairies and British Columbia, also in New York, for a few years, until his father, who was getting on in years, sent for him to come home and take over the farm.

This article from a local newspaper gives a full account of her life.

On March 4, 2003 Edith Campbell was "gathered to her people, old and full of days."

Edith was born in Little Sands on May 25, 1897–the youngest in a family of seven children born to Murdoch MacNeill and Rebecca Lamont. She attended the local school and after a time caring for an invalid sister, entered the P.E.I. School of Nursing, graduating in 1923. She was the sole survivor of her class but kept in contact with (and enjoyed visits from) the hospital alumnae over the years.

Following her graduation, she nursed for a number of years—mostly in P.E.I.—but spent periods of time nursing in both New York and Boston. She returned to the Island from Boston in 1928 and shortly thereafter married John Campbell of Uigg. Then, for a period of twenty years, she settled in to a life of farming and raising her six children. Since she was one of the few nurses in the area she was periodically called on to practice her nursing skills—both in the community and in the Montague and P.E.I. Hospitals

The family moved to Toronto in 1949 where she nursed at the Sunnybrook Veterans Hospital for a period of ten years.

After retiring to Charlottetown in 1959, she remained in her own home until she was past the hundred mark.

Her first move was to Andrew's Lodge, from there to Sunset Lodge and, when it closed, she ended her days in the Atlantic Baptist Home. In all of these homes she received attentive and loving care.

In her 104th year she was privileged to attend a special Millennium Year celebration at Government House where Seniors who had lived in three centuries were honoured. While there, a reporter asked her the secret of her longevity. She replied: " I have no secret because (and pointing at the sky) it obviously came from above–but I do appreciate the favour."

Having lived a long life she was happy to be released from these earthly bonds. For, early in life, she had come to a 'saving knowledge of the truth' and throughout her life maintained a strong faith in her Lord and Master; consequently, she fully expected to inhabit one of the Mansions prepared for His people.

She is survived by sons: Sam (Ewen), Roy, Clarence, Sheldon and daughter Eva. Her husband John predeceased her in 1964 and her daughter Rebecca (Williams) in 1978. She is fondly remembered by 14 grandchildren, numerous great grandchildren and one great-great grandchild.

The children of Edith MacNeill and John Campbell are:

D1. Samuel Ewen Campbell, spent his working career in Ontario as a locomotive engineer with the Canadian Pacific Railroad. He married Norma Trodden. They live near Smiths Falls, Ontario, and had issue:

E1. John William Campbell, m. Margaret Hayes, living near Smiths Falls, with issue:

F1. Samuel John Campbell.

F2. William Isaac Campbell.

F3. Simon Thomas Campbell.

F4. Maria Elise Campbell.

E2. Donald Kenneth Campbell, m. Ruth Coleman, living near Smiths Falls, with issue:

F1. Andrea Rebecca Campbell.

F2. Ashley Elizabeth Campbell.

F3. Abraham Samuel Campbell.

E3. Douglas James Campbell, m. Wendy Bogstie, living in Alberta, with issue:

F1. Michael Dale Campbell.

F2. David James Campbell.

F3. Amy Pearl Campbell.

E4. Marilyn Jane Campbell, m. Pierre Sincennes, living in Ontario, with issue:

F1. Nicholas Alexander Sincennes.

F2. Benjamin Samuel Sincennes.

F3. Emily Elizabeth Sincennes.

D2. Donald Roy Campbell, Ph.D., Professor and former Dean of Education at U.P.E.I., m. Maida Harris, R.N., Ontario. They live in Charlottetown, with issue:

E1. James Campbell, a Civil Engineer in Nova Scotia, m. Virginia Brown, with issue:
    F1. Corey Jean Campbell.
    F2. Derek Roy Campbell.
E2. Ian Campbell, M.D., practising in Montreal, m. Marie-Claude Marchessault, with issue:
    F1. Genevieve Marie-France Campbell.
    F2. Julien-Anne Grace Campbell.
    F3. Florence Campbell.
E3. Cathy Campbell, m. Michael Ungar, from Montreal. They live near Charlottetown, with issue:
    F1. Scott Ungar-Campbell.
    F2. Megan Ungar-Campbell.
E4. Heather Campbell, m. Joseph Driscoll. They live near Charlottetown, with issue:
    F1. Vanessa Driscoll.
    F2. Jason Driscoll.
D3. Rebecca Campbell, 1932–1978, buried in Chilliwack, B.C., m. Ronald Edgar Williams, 1931–2001. They were married in Toronto, later moved to British Columbia, and had issue:
    E1. Katherine Anne Williams, m. Jack Fleming, with issue:
        F1. Elizabeth Fleming.
        F2. David Fleming.
        F3. Rebecca Fleming.
    E2. Julia Elizabeth Williams, m. Gordon Tarras, with issue:
        F1. Jefferson Tarras.
        F2. Andrea Tarras.
    E3. Winton Williams, m. Elaine Mary, with issue:
        F1. Kimberly Sandra Williams.
        F2. Benjamin Michael Williams.

E4. Andrew James Williams, m. Karen Lee, with issue:
- F1. Collin Williams.
- F2. Mark Williams.
- F3. Carline Williams.

D4. Clarence Campbell, M.D., m. Dot Bussey, R.N., Newfoundland. They are living in Little Sands, with issue:

E1. Evelyn Campbell, R.N., m. Stephen Miller, Orthopaedic Surgeon, practising in Charlottetown, with issue:
- F1. Charlotte Louise Miller.
- F2. Jack Thomas Miller.

E2. John Campbell, M.D., practising in Nova Scotia.

D5. Sheldon Campbell, living in Charlottetown.

D6. Eva Campbell, m. Marcel Pronovost, as his second wife. He played with the Detroit Red Wings for a number of years and his name is in the Hockey Hall of Fame. He is now a scout for the New Jersey Devils hockey team. They live in Windsor, Ontario.

B7. Mary Lamont, b. 1858, died in infancy.

B8. Elizabeth Lamont, b. 1858, twin to Mary, died in infancy, one died at one week, the other at two weeks.

Mary Elizabeth Lamont

B9. Mary Elizabeth Lamont, 1860-1935, died at the home of her son, Sam Hume, Uigg. When her sister Catherine, who was living in Cambridge, Mass., at the time, was informed of her death she penned the following:

> *Tho' oft were my sighs, I shed not a tear;*
> *When I heard of my dear sister's death,*
> *For why should I weep when her rest was so sweet,*
> *As she smilingly breathed her last breath.*
> *We walked hand in hand,*
> *The strangers would ask*
> *"Little girls, which's the older of you?"*
> *We sauntered to school,*
> *We learned the same tasks;*
> *Till our childhood's short summer was through.*
> *We walked arm in arm,*
> *We talked of our beaux;*
> *When the roses were blooming most fair!*
> *Oh! youth what a charm!*
> *What enchantment she throws,*
> *O'er the love that's perfuming the air!*
> *We parted at last to our separate homes,*
> *Since that day were our meetings but rare*
> *To heaven you are gone,*
> *Sweet sister of mine;*
> *Oh! fain would I follow you there.*

Mary Lamont married John Hume, 1857-1918, son of Sam Hume, 1834-1886, age 52, Wood Islands, and Catherine Lamont d. 1914, age 79, from Belfast. Catherine was not related to the Lyndale Lamonts. John's obituary in one of the local papers reads as follows:

One of the faithful men of the P.E.I. Railway passed to his eternal reward on the 7th of May in the person of John A. Hume who was section foreman on the Murray Harbour Branch for many years. Some months ago he had a slight attack of paralysis which gradually weakened his physical power when on the above date he gently fell asleep. He was a man who will be greatly missed not only as a faithful Elder of the Church of Jesus Christ, but like the faithful sentinel, he was always at the post of duty and whether in the family, or the community, or in the congregation, he invariably stood for what he was convinced was right. For many years he was a faithful member of Jubilee L.O.L. He was in the 60th year of his age and leaves to mourn a widow, nee Mary Lamont, and the following family: Samuel, Bella, and David at home; Mrs. Donald MacIntosh, Cheadle, Alberta; Mrs. Richard MacPherson and Ewen in Butte, Montana, and Donald in the 14th Battalion in France; another son, John William, made the supreme sacrifice in France in August of last year.

Their children were:
> C1. Catherine Hume, 1885-1919 m. Richard MacPherson, her cousin. His family left the Island some years before, settling in Butte, Montana, later moving to Los Angeles. When Richard became a young man his father sent him back to the Island to select a wife rather than marry one of the California girls whom he thought were "flighty."
>
> Richard's choice was his own cousin. They were married on the Island and then spent a few days in Boston visiting relatives before leaving to make their home in California.
>
> Their children were:
>> D1. Elizabeth MacPherson, 1906-1994, m. Dallas Esdrus Ludwick, 1906-1985, with issue:
>>> E1. Betty Jean Ludwick, lives in Palm Springs,

California, and is top interpreter for the deaf in all of California. She has gone to hospitals, court rooms, has taught sign language for years in Palm Springs and Los Angeles, and at one time was called in to interpret for President George Bush.

D2. Mary MacPherson, never married, living in Sedona, Arizona.

D3. James MacPherson, m. Harriet Olcott, 1909–1990, living in Monterey Park, California, with issue:

    E1. Pamela MacPherson, m. J.R. Wagner, with one daughter:

        F1. Jennifer Wagner.

D4. Alice MacPherson, 1911–1953, m. Richard Peterson. They lived in San Fernando Valley, California, and had two daughters:

    E1. Terry Peterson, m. Richard Bennett, living in Redmond, Washington, with issue:

        F1. Kendra Bennett.

        F2. David Bennett.

    E2. Cathy Peterson, m. Hall.

D5. Harold MacPherson, M.D., 1914–2002, practised in Reno, Nevada, m. 1) Shirley Hatfield, 1926–1985, with issue:

    E1. Sandy MacPherson, m. Mike Tackett, living in Reno, Nevada, with one son:

        F1. James Tackett.

Harold married a second woman, whose name is unknown.

D6. Dorothy MacPherson, 1919–1977, m. Paul Ervine. They lived in La Cresenta, California, and had two daughters:

    E1. Andrea Ervine, m. John Williams, living in La Cresenta.

E2. Eileen Ervine, m. Curt Simpson, living in Huntington Beach, California.

D7. Isabella MacPherson, m. James Simerly, living in Fresno, California. They had three children:

E1. Dianne Simerly, m. David Cloyd, living in Clovis, California, with two daughters:

F1. Starr Ann Cloyd.

F2. Ruth Cloyd, m. _____ Jenson.

E2. David Simerly, m. Janine Syll, living in Mill Valley, California, with two children:

F1. Kyle Simerly.

F2. Sean Mac Simerly.

E3. Richard Simerly, m. Nancy Sayre, living in Tigard, Oregon, with issue:

F1. Kathryn Simerly.

F2. Eric Simerly.

C2. Ewen Hume, December 22, 1887–1969, m. Prudence Amelia Taylor, daughter of Capt. William Taylor, Wood Islands and Millview. They lived in Butte, Montana for a few years, where he worked as a carpenter in the mines. A few of their children were born there. He came back to Canada and farmed for three years in Lyndale, next to his uncle Malcolm Lamont's farm, before returning to Massachusetts where he followed the carpentry trade. They had issue:

D1. William Ewen Hume, m. _____, with issue:

E1. Penelope Taylor Hume, m. Weston Allen Baker. They live in Auburn, Maine, and have issue:

F1. Leith Baker.

F2. Katie Baker.

D2. Mary Alice Hume, won a substantial prize for a literary work she had submitted to the Boston *Globe*. She m. James Buzzell, no family.

D3. John Alexander Hume, m. Mary MacIntyre.

They lived in Mass. and had issue:
- E1. Carol Hume, married.
- E2. John Hume, married.
- E3. Tommy Hume, married.
- E4. Allen Hume, married

D4. Lloyd Hume, baptized December 9th, 1923, never married, living in Somerville, Mass.

D5. Elmer Hume, baptized December 9th, 1923, m. Priscilla Allen. They lived in Hingham, Mass., with issue:
- E1. Debby Hume, m. 1) _____ Howe, with issue:
    - F1. Heidi Howe.

    Debby m. 2) Charles Stockbridge, living in Scituate, Mass., with issue:
    - F2. Rebecca Stockbridge, married.
    - F3. Lindsay Stockbridge, married.
    - F4. Charles Stockbridge.
- E2. Sandra Hume, m. Ray Bailey, living in Virginia, with issue:
    - F1. Meredith Bailey.
    - F2. Kimberly Bailey.
    - F3. A boy, died young.
- E3. Donald Hume, not married, living in Plymouth, Mass.

D6. Isabella Hume, m. Charles Gordon Mood, with issue:
- E1. Cheryl Karen Mood, m. Gary Lee Ogden.
- E2. Gordon Leslie Mood, m. Anne-Marie Stephenson.
- E3. Karen Gail Mood.
- E4. Donna Louise Mood.
- E5. Charles Wayne Mood, m. Angelia Phyllis Abbate.

D7. Gladys Dorothy Hume, m. Harold Emmet Mood, with issue:

E1. William Robert Mood.
   E2. Stephen David Mood.
   E3. Diana Lee Mood.
   E4. Richard Bradley Mood.
   E5. Susan Nancy Mood.
   E6. David Mood.
D8. Richard Hume, m. Winnifred Carisle, from Maine. They are retired and living in Vero Beach, Florida, their children are:
   E1. Wendy Hume, m. Robert Lundell, living in Mass.
   E2. Richard Scott Hume, m. 1) Sandy King, from Baltimore, with issue:
      F1. Jessica Hume.
   Richard m. 2) Jean MacDonald, with issue:
      F2. Richard Hume.
      F3. Brandon Hume.
   Richard m. 3) Teresa Bradford, with issue:
      F4. Allison Hume.
D9. Robert Hume, m. Anne Armand, living in Mass., with issue:
   E1. Robert Hume, m. Carol _____, living in Mass., with issue:
      F1. Nicholas Hume.
      F2. Michael Hume.
   E2. James Hume, m. Morgan _____, living in Arizona, with issue:
      F1. James Hume, called JT.
   E3. Linda Hume, m. ____ Chagnon, with issue:
      F1. Jessica Chagnon.
      F2. Sarah Hume.
   E4. Donna Hume, m. Don Harty, living in Mass., with issue:
      F1. Aaron Harty.
      F2. Jeri Harty.

E5. Laura Hume, had issue:
   F1. Jillian Hume.
Laura m. 1) _____ Tubert, with issue:
   F2. Shawn Tubert.
Laura m. 2) Michael Walanski, with issue:
   F3. Trevor Walanski.

Donald MacIntosh and Sarah Hume

C3. Sarah Margaret Hume, 1889–1968, m. Donald MacIntosh, 1884–1975, from Stanchel, P.E.I. (their mothers were sisters). Their family is listed under Frances Lamont and Alexander MacIntosh.

There is an interesting history of this family written by their daughter, Lillian MacIntosh Ross.

C4. Samuel Hume, 1891-1967, m. Edith Campbell, 1898–1990, daughter of Donald Campbell and Flora MacLeod, Uigg. They took over her father's farm in Uigg and had one son:

D1. Donald Hume, 1921–1944, who was in the Armed Services was killed in an air crash in Labrador during WWII. He was married to Katherine Shaw, daughter of Ernest Shaw and Murdina MacLeod, Uigg. They had one son:
    E1. John Hume, m. Linda Bierens. They live near Charlottetown, and have two children:
        F1. Cathy Hume, m. Sheldon Stewart. They live in Summerside, P.E.I., with two children:
            G1. Alyssa Stewart.
            G2. Braeden Stewart.
        F2. Donald Hume, m. Kelly Anne Smyth, daughter of Blaine and Kaye Smyth, living in Truro, Nova Scotia, with two children:
            G1. Ethan Hume.
            G2. Kieren Hume.
C5. Isabella Hume, 1894–1923, died in Boston, buried in Belle River cemetery.
C6. John Willie Hume, 1895-1916, was wounded at Courcelette, France, and died two days later.

When John Willie was serving in France in WWI his father had a stroke leaving him bedfast with a loss of speech for a time. One day he signalled his wife, and family who were home at that time, to sing a particular Psalm from the Psalter. While they were singing, John Willie's voice came in, loud and clear, singing along with them. A few days later they received a message from the War Office informing them that he was killed from enemy action.

    Norman MacDonald, Nine Mile Creek, tells of when he was also in the front lines in France during WWI. They were sleeping in tents. On one particular evening, at dusk, he heard someone, in another tent farther up the line, singing a "MacDonaldite" hymn that he was familiar with and heard in his own church since a boy:

> *We hail with joy the dawning morn,*
> *The love of God shall soon be shown;*
> *The tribes afar, with joy shall hear,*
> *Messiah comes, redemption's near.*

Norman said to himself, "These are my people, I am going up to see who they are." It was John Willie Hume, from Wood Islands.

In Catherine Lamont Hume's scrapbook we find the following:

> *Dear John Willie thou hast fallen*
> *On the distant battlefield.*
> *But thy work on earth was finished*
> *And to death thou needs must yield.*
> *Through many weary months of fighting*
> *Thou hast nobly played thy part*
> *In defence of right and justice*
> *Marching forth with fearless heart.*
> *Oh how sadly we remember*
> *The last time you marched away*
> *But 'twas duty called thee onward*
> *And we could not bid thee stay*
> *Many prayers for thee we've offered*
> *Many silent tears we've shed.*

C7. Elizabeth Hume, 1897–1912, died at age 14 years.
C8. Donald Hume, 1899-1937, served overseas in World War One, m. Edith Stillman. He was killed by a boiler explosion when working in a factory in Toronto. He left a young family:
    D1. Aaron Hume, m. Phyllis Kinck, living in Toronto, with issue:
        E1. Michael Hume, m. Cathy _____, with issue:
        F1. Joshua Hume.

F2. Johanna Hume.
E2. Jeffery Hume, m. Shawn _____, with issue:
F1. Matthew Hume.
F2. Kathleen Hume.
E3. Judy Hume, nurse at Sick Children's Hospital, Toronto.
E4. Derek Hume, married, in Toronto.
D2. Stuart Hume, died 1966, age 35, m. Margaret Miller, she died aged 41. They had issue:
E1. Donald Hume, m. Jo-Anne _____, with issue
F1. Stacy Hume.
D3. Bruce Hume, died young in Glace Bay, Nova Scotia.
D4. George Hume, m. Mary Elizabeth Brown, with issue:
E1. Karen Elizabeth Hume.
E2. Linda Diane Hume.
E3. Marla Anne Hume.
E4. Colin Hume.
E5. Sean Hume, twin to Colin above.
C9. David Hume, 1902 ____, last thought to be living in California.

Catherine Lamont

B10. Catherine Lamont, b. 1862, daughter of Ewen Lamont and Sarah MacPherson, Lyndale, was a school teacher. She married Joseph Hume, 1864–1925, Brooklyn, P.E.I., where they lived for a time before moving to Mass. The following is his obituary, which appeared in the local paper:

Passed suddenly and peacefully to his everlasting rest on Sabbath the 15th of November, 1925, Joseph S. Hume of Cambridge and formerly of Brooklyn, P.E.I. Mr. Hume was in his usual health until the morning of his death and having risen early as was his wont, he was suddenly seized with some heart affection, which continued only for an hour, when he calmly fell asleep. It was remembered that he had frequently uttered both the prediction and the desire that he should receive his heavenly call without a prolonged illness.

Deceased was a convert of what was known as the Third Revival in the Church of Scotland on P.E.I. passing through soul experiences that were both remarkable and abiding. He was many years an Elder in the Church of Scotland where the tenderness of his prayers and the rich compass of his voice in the praises of the sanctuary will be long remembered and missed.

Deceased is survived by his widow Catherine, daughter of the late Ewen Lamont of Lyndale, P.E.I., by one son, Ewen, an officer in the U.S. Navy, by five daughters, Emily, Mrs. Kidston; Sarah, Mrs. Stymeist; Margaret, Mrs. MacMillan; Elizabeth, Mrs. MacDougall; Florence, Mrs. MacNevin and by sixteen grandchildren.

They had issue:
- C1. Emily Hume, b. 1886, m. William Kidston, in the U.S.A., with issue:
  - D1. Emma Jean Kidston, b. 1911.
  - D2. Catherine Kidston, b. 1912.
  - D3. Jessie Kidston, b. 1914.
  - D4. William Arthur Kidston, b. 1918.
  - D5. Teddy Louis Kidston, b. 1920.
- C2. Sarah Frances Hume, 1888–1972, m. 1) William Stymeist, 1884–1934, Murray River. They lived in Mass., with issue:
  - D1. Edmond Stymeist, 1907-1960, m. 1) Ellie Compton, 2) Betty Harrington, no family.
  - D2. Joseph Sanders Stymeist, 1910-1974, a clergy-

man, m. Ronda Keown, with issue:
- E1. David Stymeist.
- E2. John Stymeist.

D3. John Thomas Stymeist, 1912–1940, m. Eleanor Austin:
- E1. Marcia Stymeist, m. Jerry Williams, with issue:
  - F1. Jenny Williams, m. Joe Neal, with issue:
    - G1. Patrick Neal.
  - F2. Chris Williams.

D4. William Amos Stymeist, II, 1915-1962, m. 1) Frances Westgate, with issue:
- E1. Sandra Stymeist.
- E2. William Amos Stymeist, III, 1934–1998, m. Jean Schramm, with issue:
  - F1. Denyse Stymeist.
  - F2. Steven Stymeist.
  - F3. Colleen Stymeist.
  - F4. Melody Stymeist.

William Amos, II, m. 2) Betty ___, 1909–1974, with issue:
- E3. Robert Stymeist.

William Amos, II, m. 3) Eleanor Mabin, with issue:
- E4. John William Steymeist, 1950–1972.
- E5. Joseph Gerard Stymeist, m. Louise Dobeck, with issue:
  - F1. Melissa Louise Stymeist.
  - F2. Amanda Jo Stymeist.
- E6. Edward Allen Stymeist, m. Linda Wethington, with issue:
  - F1. Janelle Nicolle Stymeist.
- E7. Barbara Jean Stymeist, m. James Golden, with issue:
  - F1. James Golden.
  - F2. Grant Golden.

D5. Jessie Emiline Stymeist, 1917-1982, m. 1) Bert Bennett, with issue:
    E1. JoAnne Rachel Bennett.
    E2. William Richard Bennett.
    E3. Betty Lou Bennett.
    E4. James Bennett.
    E5. John Bennett.
    E6. Sally Bennett, m. Roco Scally.
Jessie Emiline Stymeist, m. 2) ____ Curtis.
D6. Alexander Munroe Stymeist (Buddy), 1922-1978, m. Dorothy Piper, 1919–1991. They lived in Mass., with issue:
    E1. Theodore Munroe Stymeist, m. Shirley Ann Evans.
    E2. Lou Stymeist, m. Brian Goodman.
D7. Betty Catherine Stymeist, 1927–1992, m. Joseph Savage. They lived in Texas, with issue:
    E1. Jason Savage.
    E2. Joseph Savage.
    E3. John Savage.
    E4. James Savage.
    E5. Jeff Savage.
    E6. Sarah Savage.
C3. Margaret Hume, b. 1891, m. Allan MacMillan, Mass., U.S.A.
C4. Elizabeth Hume, b. 1892, m. Edmond MacDougall, 1885–1943, Bangor, P.E.I., where they farmed for a few years before moving to Mass.. They adopted a boy while in Bangor:
    D1. Lester B. MacDougall, m. Irene Norris, with issue:
        E1. Linda Joyce MacDougall, m. Jack W. Corzine, with issue:
            F1. Christopher Scott Corzine.
            F2. Jeffrey Allan Corzine.

F3. Julie Beth Corzine.
E2. Jeffrey Scott MacDougall, m. Karen Roberts, with issue:
F1. Scott Gregory MacDougall.
F2. Tyler Roberts MacDougall.
C5. David Hume, 1895–1913, his obituary appeared in a Boston newspaper as follows:

Deepest Sympathy will be extended to Joseph and Mrs Hume, Cambridge, Mass., in the death of their eldest well-beloved son David, who passed peacefully to his eternal rest on the morning of January 3rd, 1913, at the early age of 18. He had been in the Cambridge Hospital for eight days where he underwent an operation for appendicitis, but medical and surgical treatment were of no avail, as his appendix was ruptured and he developed blood poisoning; his death comes as a severe shock to his parents and wide circle of home friends. At an early age he was awakened from the grave of "spiritual death," in the "Revival meetings" in the Church of Scotland, Cambridge, Mass., and although that spark of life which had been kindled appeared to be dim, still the flax was smoking until he was brought down upon a bed of affliction of soul and body. He endured his sufferings with great patience and was upheld by God's grace and favour as found in Jesus Christ, whom he knew as his Saviour, on Him who is the "Bread of Life," his soul was able to feed, and thus partaking of Him, he was sustained in spirit during the severest distress. His death bed shall never be forgotten by those who visited him, for his heart was filled with love, and his mind with thoughts of his eternal welfare, and he advised those younger than himself to "seek the Lord while He is to be found and call upon Him while He is near, for He is rich in mercy, so kind and loving, that a bruised reed He will not break and smoking flax He will not quench." He was sunshine in his home, ambitious and lovable, and the sweet consoling message he left was "don't fret, think of me rejoicing in Glory."

His mother, in her grief at the loss of her son, penned the following:

The Pall

Deep mantle in whose folds are only sighs
Light is changed to darkness, day is night
There is no light.
Strains of music ne'er so clear
Fall deadly on the listless ear
Floral wreaths may bloom, may die
Unnoticed by the tear dimmed eye.

Comforts that love dares impart
Ne'er soothes, ne'er ease the broken heart.
A voice from heaven breaks the spell
"Your child is safe and all is well"
I shout aloud Amen! Amen!!
I'll see my darling boy again!!!

C6. Ewen Hume, 1898–1939, was a Naval Officer in the U.S.A. In the Los Angeles National cemetery we find: Hume, Ewen Lamont, d. 12/29/1939, Chief Fire Controlman, USN, Plot: 95 6, bur. 01/05/1940. He was married to Margaret Jane Compton, daughter of Lemuel Compton and Lucy Anne Compton, Belle River. Ewen and Margaret had issue:

    D1. Margaret Frances Hume, m. Patrick Joseph Roach, Mass., with issue:

        E1. Lorraine Roach.

        E2. Pat Roach, m. Fred Dupont.

C7. Florence Nightingale Hume, b. 1902, m. Charles

MacNevin. They had issue:
   D2. Joseph MacNevin, b. 1921.
   D1. Christine MacNevin, b. 1923.
C8. John S. Hume, 1905-1905.

Rev. Murdoch Lamont

B11. Rev. Murdoch Lamont, 1865-1928, was a clergyman in the Church of Scotland. Author of *The Life and Times of the Rev. Donald MacDonald*. He married Euphemia Ann Hume, 1866-1934, from Wood Islands, sister of John Hume, married to his sister Mary. They farmed in Lyndale for a few years before moving to Stanchel, later moving to Massachusetts, where he worked at the carpentry trade for a short time before studying for the ministry in the Church of Scotland. Despite being older, and having the care of a wife and seven children, when beginning University studies, yet he won a scholarship to Edinburgh University that was open to students from all over the British Empire.

His obituary in a local paper reads:

Rev. Murdoch Lamont

News has just arrived from Scotland that the Rev. Murdoch Lamont, formerly of Prince Edward Island, has closed his ministry in the Church on earth and entered into his rest and reward on the 13th August, 1927, at the age of 62.

Mr. Lamont, after an attack of heart weariness, died peacefully in his home, tenderly comforted by his family. His sons, Mr. Ewen Lamont, M.A. and professor William D. Lamont of Glasgow University, happened to be at home on a visit. Mr. Lamont, after a strenuous week of pastoral work came home on Saturday evening and complained of some heart affection. He immediately retired to his bed and soon after peacefully fell asleep in Jesus. He had only returned a few days previous from a preaching mission among the fishermen of the Western Isles.

Mr. Lamont's life, if written, would present a record of hardships faced and difficulties surmounted that would read like a romance. He was a carpenter, busy at his trade in Boston, when he became convinced of his call to the ministry. But he was over 40 and he had a large family of eight depending on his income.

Few ever enter an Old Country University at his age. And his sudden decision to study for the Church of Scotland and cross the Atlantic with such a family, and no visible means of support, seemed to come not so much an act of faith as a daring of Providence. He crossed to Scotland, nevertheless, and on his arrival, Providence seemed to link him up immediately into a chain of coincidences that enabled him to reach the objective of his calling. But what struggles, what domestic privations! Half of the credit for his successes is due to his faithful wife, who shared with him and braved with him, in all his trials. Two links in that chain of coincidences, Mr. Lamont himself spoke of as Divine ruling. First, when the time for his matriculation into the University of Glasgow had come and when the prospect for his entrance seemed blackest, suddenly the assistantship of the famous old St. Columba Church became vacant. Mr. Lamont was introduced to the trustees and was asked to preach for the congregation, with the result that he was unanimously chosen. But the salary was far from adequate for the payment of college fees and the support of a numerous household. Yet what a solid standing and substantial support this appointment meant to the struggling student— old, even beyond his years.

But his little boys were helping out in their eager little ways. And would it not have astonished him had he been told when trudging to the University with his bundle of books, that one day one of those little boys of his, who were selling newspapers to help out, would ere long be professor of philosophy in that same University?

Meanwhile, present difficulties were all-engrossing; but when prospects were once more at their darkest, once more relief was at hand. A scholarship of considerable financial value was flung open for competition to the four Universities of Scotland. Mr. Lamont at once took up the challenge. And although he was already saddled with the double labour of fulfilling the ministry in St. Columba, and his tasks for the University, he nevertheless entered the lists.

The result was announced in the Oban *Times*:

> Mr. Lamont, a Glasgow student, has been awarded the MacKenzie Scholarship, founded by Miss Eliza B. MacKenzie in memory of her brother, Rev. J. MacKenzie, minister of Kettins. This scholarship was open to all Divinity students of all the Universities of Scotland. Mr. Lamont's essay is on "The Charter of Presbytery, the Act of 1592, its Origin and History."

This placed Mr. Lamont and his family on "easy street."

But he had no sooner finished college and began his work as a parish minister in Islay than another calamity darkened the skies. The Great War broke out upon the world. Mr. Lamont's three sons were called to the colours. The father was asked to give his written consent, for one of them was under age. This he readily gave. Not only so, but he himself, being a skillful mechanic, entered a munitions factory where he laboured day and night, while preaching every Sabbath. So that he and his three sons and also his only brother in Scotland, Rev. D.M. Lamont, who had been appointed under the Admiralty a chaplain to the Internal Prisoners of War, were all and at the same time "doing their bit."

Mr. Murdoch Lamont's ministry before and after ordination, extended well over twenty years. To the end he remained vigorous in mind and body. In the biographical history of the Christian Church, many of God's labourers have prayed that they might die in harness. This divine favour fell to Mr. Lamont. He was spared the discomforts of old age. He never had to endure prolonged sickness. It is significant that one of Mr. Lamont's sermons was from the text: "The Lord Whom ye seek shall suddenly come to His temple." And at the conclusion of his sermon on this text, as if anticipating his own sudden call, he remarked, "As for ourselves, He suddenly called us in to this world, and He will suddenly call us away." This was nearly his last sermon and sounded like a premonition. But his last recorded subject was on Thanksgiving. Like many of the older ministers, he kept a journal of his life from his 'teens, covering a period of over forty years. And his last message was a befitting farewell on the text, "Now unto the King Eternal, Immortal, Invisible, the only wise God be honour and glory for ever and ever, Amen."

Mr. Lamont used often to say of his own ministry, "My highest ambition is to be a humble link in the great chain of men and events that are advancing the glorious kingdom of Jesus Christ."

He is survived by his widow, Effie Ann, daughter of the late Sam Hume of Wood Islands, by his sons, Sam, Ewen, Donald, William, Malcolm, David, and by his daughters, Katie (Mrs. Dr. Jack), Mrs. Wilson and Murdina (Mrs. Stewart); also by brothers, Malcolm, Donald M., minister on P.E.I., and sisters, Mrs. MacIntosh, Mrs. MacNeill, Mrs. John Hume and Mrs. Joseph Hume.

It may be added that Mr. Lamont, shortly before his death, lectured before the Eccles. Soc. of the Church of Scotland in Edinburgh. This lecture was much spoken of and he was urged to publish it, and it is believed he has left the manuscript in suitable form for publication. His first published work was "Rev. D. MacDonald, His Life and Times," a very candid and impartial history. Many of the translations in the MacDonaldite Hymn Book are from his pen.

Murdoch kept a diary for most of his adult life. Copied from the last page of his diary and written some weeks before his death is the following:

> April 30th 1927
>
> Today I enter my 63rd year. Soon the figures of my full age will fit the rhyme we used to sing at Lyndale School:
> "I'm an old old man, just come from the war, just come from the war, I'm an old old man just come from the war, my age is sixty and three."
> I enter my 63rd year in very good health; and thankful to the giver of all good, but now it often strikes me that the things I do will outlast me. I thought of it today as I was finishing a garden gate.
> I think of it when writing my session records, it affects my planning for the future. I anticipate now less romance in my life since the most of it is past. At the same time there is a calm, less worry about the future, more trust in the hand that never grows old, never errs, ever ruling all things and all events. To translate a couplet of a Gaelic psalm:
> "My courage all would vanish quite, could I God's goodness doubt." M.L.

The children of Rev. Murdoch Lamont and Effie Anne Hume were:

    C1. Samuel Lamont, b. 1890, m. Lillian Taylor, daughter of Capt. William Taylor, Wood Islands and Millview. They were married in Butte, Montana, September 25th, 1912, but later moved to British Columbia and had issue:

        D1. Lillian Lamont, m. 1) _____ MacPherson,

with issue:
    E1. Thelma Ann MacPherson.
    E2. Michael MacPherson.
Lillian m. 2) _____ Lanegraff, 3) Robert Bateman, with issue:
    E3. Ellen Lanegraff.
D2. Samuel Lamont, married in British Columbia, with issue:
    E1. Robert Lamont, married in B.C. with two children.
    E2. Allen Lamont.
C2. Frances Lamont, b. 1891, died young.
C3. Sarah Ann Lamont, 1892-1983, m. Dr. R.P. Jack, Birmingham, England, with issue:
    D1. Mary Jack, not living, never married.
    D2. Donald Jack 1924-1991, m. Nancy Tollhurst, d. 1991, with issue:
        E1. Maren Jack, m. _____ Padwick, with three children.
        E2. Louise Jack (Lulu), m. _____ Hilton, with three children.
A tribute to the career of Donald Jack appeared in the Toronto *Globe and Mail*:

Once in the middle of an interview at the Toronto airport, writer Donald Jack left to fetch a document from his car. Notorious for a sense of direction so poor he found it difficult to navigate through a city park, let alone the airport's massive parking lot. Mr. Jack took so long to find his vehicle that by the time he returned the interviewers had gone.

Like Bartholomew Bandy, the hapless hero of *The Bandy Papers*, Mr. Jack's eight-volume comic-novel series describing an Ottawa Valley boy's adventures during both world wars and between, the author often found himself in hilarious situations, made the more so by his telling.

A three-time winner of the Stephen Leacock Memorial Medal for Humour, Mr. Jack died last week at his home in England. He was 78.

Listeners were reduced to tears of laughter by his tales of construction disasters while having a villa built in Spain; a house sale falling through on closing day; and an aging bright yellow car named Buttercup, whose sun roof shattered soon after it was searched for drugs at the Spanish-French border, showering Mr. Jack with glass, insects and rust. Once, while being toured with daughter around the offices of his publisher, McClelland & Stewart, Mr. Jack entered the boardroom and shouted with surprise. There on the carpet lay a large amount of dog excrement left by an employee's pet. In his Bandy-like way, the writer very nearly stepped into it. "If you could choose one author out of the entire world who during a visit to his publisher would stumble across this, it would be Donald Jack," said Douglas Gibson, president and publisher of McClelland & Stewart, who knew the writer for more than 30 years.

"Things would go wrong for Don, very seldom caused by himself," said Munroe Scott, a close friend of more than 45 years. "He would narrate all this stuff either in person or in a letter and make it all hilarious, because he always saw, in retrospect at any rate, the funny side of things. You'd be doubled up with laughter."

Despite Mr. Jack's incident-prone nature, it would be a mistake to see Mr. Jack as a buffoon, said Mr. Scott, also a writer. "He was enormously well read, erudite and could handle the language with aplomb at many levels. He could make me feel like a Philistine," said author Austin Clarke, who was Mr. Jack's neighbour for five years during the 1960s. "He was a quiet, reserved, retiring kind of man. You would never have known he was a writer."

Mr. Jack's Leacock medals came for three volumes of *The Bandy Papers*: *Three Cheers for Me*, in 1963, *That's*

Me in the Middle, in 1974, and *Me Bandy, You Cissie*, in 1980. Published between 1963 and 1996. They still enjoy a loyal following, including a Web site which draws mail from around the world. Six of the eight volumes were recently reissued by McClelland & Stewart.

Drawn from Mr. Jack's fascination with the First World War, the rural people he met in the Ottawa Valley and his time in the Royal Air Force, *The Bandy Papers* feature the blundering Bartholomew Wolfe Bandy, who in the first volume, *Three Cheers for Me*, inadvertently becomes a hero, despite capturing his own colonel by mistake. Ensuing volumes follow Mr. Bandy's adventures through to the Second World War. Although devastatingly funny. They also describe war's horrors and the realities of the home front, and lampoon war's leaders.

Mr. Bandy encounters and influences historical figures, such as then British minister of defence Winston Churchill, and generously offers him use of the altered Bandy phrase "blood, sweat, toil and tears." While best known for *The Bandy Papers*, Mr. Jack wrote countless film scripts, TV and radio plays, as well as two non-fiction books: the history of a Toronto radio station, *Sinc, Betty and the Morning Man*, and another about medicine in Canada, *Rogues, Rebels and Geniuses*.

His third play, *The Canvas Barricade*, won first prize in the Stratford Shakespearean Play Writing Competition in 1960. Produced in 1961, it was the first, and remains the only, original Canadian play performed in the main stage of the Stratford Festival. Mr. Jack, however, did not see much of its opening. He left the auditorium for the lobby. "During the performance, we'd be aware of a crack of light from a door opening slightly and a white face would stare through, then vanish for a while, before another door would open a crack, and the same apparition would fleetingly appear," Mr. Scott said.

Born on Dec. 8, 1924, in Radcliffe, Lancashire, England, Donald Lamont Jack was one of four children of a British doctor and nurse from Prince Edward Island [Sarah Ann Lamont]. After attending Bury Grammar School in Lancashire and Marr College in Scotland, he gained enough qualifications to attend London University.

While stationed in Germany with the RAF in the last year of the Second World War, Mr. Jack attempted short-story writing, but thought he lacked talent. After his mother asked him, "Isn't it about time you left home?" Mr. Jack immigrated to Canada in 1951. Interspersed with jobs as a member of a surveying crew in Alberta and a bank teller in Toronto, Mr. Jack studied at the Canadian Theatre School in Toronto run by Sterndale Bennett. There he wrote two plays, one of which drew praise from theatre critic Nathan Cohen and a job offer from a film company. Mr. Cohen later wrote Mr. Scott, decrying Canadian theatre's "shameful treatment" of Mr. Jack, which largely ignored him. A theatrical background enhances Mr. Jack's writing, according to Mr. Gibson. "His dialogue was terrific and his scene-setting was excellent."

After leaving the school, with the encouragement of his wife, Nancy, whom he married in 1952, Mr. Jack worked in the script department of Crawley Films in Ottawa. Two years later in 1955, the company's head, Budge Crawley, let him go because he thought Mr. Jack would never make a good writer.

A dry year of freelancing followed, until in 1957 Mr. Jack sold the play version of his novelette *Breakthrough*, published in Maclean's to CBC Television. It became the first Canadian TV play to be simultaneously telecast to the United States. He never looked back. By 1972, *A Collection of Canadian Plays*, Vol. 1, which included *Exit Muttering* by Mr. Jack, noted he had written 40 TV plays, 35 documentary film scripts, several radio plays and four stage plays.

The works included Royal Canadian Navy and Canadian Armed Forces training films for the National Film Board and often demanded a great deal of research.

Mr. Jack wrote with military disciple, beginning at 9 a.m., taking tea at 11 a.m., lunch at 1 p.m., tea again at 3 p.m. and finishing at 5 p.m. "All my life, I swear, that routine never altered," said one of his daughters, Lulu Hilton.

Persisting in writing drafts in pen and ink long before adopting he typewriter and, much later, a word processor, Mr. Jack often developed story lines while walking. A 1959 CBC press release explains Mr. Jack's dedication: "My self-discipline is to keep reminding myself of how lucky I am to be able to be the only thing I ever wanted to be—a writer."

During the early 1980s, Mr. Jack and his wife returned to England to be near their daughters who had emigrated there, and their grandchildren. Mr. Jack missed Canada's open spaces and its classless society, and visited often.

At the time of his death, he was working on the ninth volume of *The Bandy Papers*. He died on or about June 2 of a massive stroke in his home in Telford, Shropshire, England. He leaves his two daughters, Maren and Lulu, six grandchildren and one great-grandchild, a brother and a sister. His wife Nancy died in 1991.

    D3. Marjorie Jack, m. Derek Honeybourne, living in Worcester, England, with issue:
        E1. Patricia Honeybourne, m. _____ Whittaker.
        E2. Amanda Honeybourne, m. _____ Hollowell, three children.
    D4. Robert M. Jack, now living in Algarve, Portugal, m. 1) Eunice Lofthouse, who died in 1990. They had issue:
        E1. Nicholas Martin Lamont Jack.
    Robert m. 2) Johanne Cardin.

C4. Katherine Belle Lamont, b. 1894, m. W. Wilson Scott, with issue.
    D1. Ronald Scott.
Katherine died in Canada when on a visit to her son. Rev. James MacGowan, a Presbyterian minister, from Kilmuir P.E.I., who was pastoring in Ontario, at the time, was asked to conduct the funeral service. He learned to his surprise that she was a descendant of the Lamonts of Lyndale.
C5. Ewen Lamont, 1896–1969, was a piper in the First World War, later attended Glasgow University, and was headmaster in a school in Glasgow. He m. Anne Tomison, with issue:
    D1. Elspeth Lamont, m. James Cleland, living in Perth, Scotland. They had issue:
        E1. Robert Cleland, m. Julie Brown, with issue:
            F1. Kate Cleland.
            F2. Eilidh Cleland.
            F3. Kirsty Cleland.
        E2. Alan Cleland, m. Heather Murray, with issue:
            F1. Briony Cleland.
            F2. Murray Cleland.
        E3. Millar Cleland, m. 1) Elaine Simpson, 2) Jackie Penny. He has three children:
            F1. Martin Cleland.
            F2. Rachael Cleland.
            F3. JoAnne Cleland.
    D2. Ewen Lamont, m. Aileen Currie, with issue:
        E1. David Lamont.
        E2. Rhona Lamont.
    D3. Thelma Lamont, m. Charles Robertson, with issue:
        E1. David Robertson, m. Linda Moug, with issue:

  F1. Hannah Robertson.
  F2. Alice Robertson.
  F3. Flora Robertson.
 E2. Neil Robertson has three children:
  F1. Maelle Robertson.
  F2. Calum Robertson.
  F3. Noa Robertson.
 E3. Colin Robertson, m. Jo Thomson, with issue:
  F1. William Robertson.
  F2. Madeleine Robertson.

C6. Donald Lamont, b. 1899, served in the armed services during the First World War. He lived in British Columbia, never married.

C7. William Dawson Lamont, 1901-1982, was born in Stanchel, P.E.I. He was at one time Principal of Makerere University, which is now one of the largest universities in East and Central Africa, with a student population of over 20,000. He also served as British Advisor to the Egyptian Government with the status of Ambassador. He is author of *The Early History of Islay*, and was married to Anne Fraser Christ, whom he met when they both attended Oxford University. They had no family.

C8. Malcolm Lamont, b. 1904, was born in Massachusetts and moved to Scotland with his parents in 1905. After he married he returned to the U.S.A., where he spent his working career as partner of more than one business. He is buried in Los Altos, California. He m. 1) Angusina MacDonald, with issue, 2) Michelle _____. Children from Angusina are:
 D1. Donald Ian Lamont, m. Betty Banner, from Virginia, with issue:
  E1. Elizabeth Lamont, m. _____, no family.
  E2. Virginia Lamont, m. Jeff Clark, from Iowa,

with issue:
    F1. Thomas Clark.
    F2. Jared Clark.
D2. Catriona Margaret Lamont (Caris), living in Los Altos, California, m. Brice DeGanahl, with issue:
    E1. Donald Andrew DeGanahl, m. _____, no family.
    E2. Sheila DeGanahl, m. Rolf Moeller, no issue.
    E3. Wendy DeGanahl, m. Nabil Keilani, with issue:
        F1. Reema Keilani.
        F2. Nadia Keilani.
    E4. Carl Brice DeGanahl, not married.
C9. David Henry Lamont, 1908–1998, author of the book titled *To Stand and Stare*, a story of his growing up in Mull, Scotland. He m. Grace Miller in 1936, whom he had met when both attended Glasgow University. After the war they moved to Uganda for a few years where David was a Social Welfare Officer. In 1949, a son was born to them in Scotland, whom they named Graeme. They separated shortly after, and in 1950 she moved back to Uganda, and later lived in Nairobi, Kenya, where she worked as manager for an insurance company. In 1952 she married 2) James Martin. Because of unsettled conditions in Kenya they moved to Australia in 1965, where Graeme adopted the surname Martin. Grace died in 1996 and James in 1997. Graeme is now living in Tasmania, where he is a computer programmer.
    D1. Graeme Martin, m. Frances Heritage. They have a daughter:
        E1. Hannah Martin, attending University in Melbourne, Australia. She is fluent in several languages.

C10. Murdina Lamont (Ena), 1912-1998, m. Jack Stewart. They lived in Scotland where she was a journalist and playwright. Two plays she had written, among others, were very successful. One was *Starched Aprons*. Another, *Men Should Weep*, is a highly successful production presented at the Glasgow Citizens' Theatre, a repertory group. Murdina and Jack had one son:
    D1. William Ewen Stewart, m. Katherine _____, with issue:
        E1. Two sons.

Rev. Donald MacDonald Lamont

B12. Rev. Donald MacDonald Lamont, 1867-1942, also studied for the ministry in Scotland and was the author of: *The History of Strath, Seven Great Questions*, and *Our Friends After Death*, also a number of poems; "The Dying Girl," "The Third Revival," "Granny's Spinning Wheel," etc. He held parishes in the Isle of Skye, Mull, and the mainland of Scotland. He also ministered in Toronto, Ontario, Dunvegan, Ontario, and the Central Parish on Prince Edward Island, before going back to Scotland to minister in Dervaig, Mull, in the famous church with the pencil spire.

A Scottish newspaper wrote of him:

> The Rev. Donald Lamont, Strath Parish, Isle of Skye, is one of the most distinguished of Highland Clergymen. An earnest minister of the Gospel and a splendid worker for the cause which he professes to teach. The most remarkable thing about Mr. Lamont however, is that being a native of Prince Edward Island, Canada, he learned all his Gaelic before he ever saw Scotland, being called only a year or two back from Canada to Rothesay where he preached with great acceptance. He is now however, placed in a much larger

sphere of usefulness. His present church is seated for 1,100 and we have no doubt that there will be few empty seats when Mr. Lamont's capabilities are known.

His obituary, in a local paper, reads:

Death of the Rev. D.M. Lamont, M.A., M.D. (Glasgow)

The Reverend Donald MacDonald Lamont, a minister of the Church of Scotland, well known in the Highlands of Scotland and Eastern Canada, died at the house of his son in Glasgow, Scotland, on the 31st May, 1942. His last charge was the parish of Kilninian, and Kilmore, Mull, from which he retired about a year ago in consequence of his declining health. By a curious coincidence, Mr. Lamont's funeral in Glasgow occurred on the day fixed for the induction of his successor in Mull. The induction of the new minister was therefore preceded by a memorial service for his predecessor.

Mr. Lamont came of old Highland stock. In the fifteenth century his branch of Clan Lamont settled in the Isle of Skye, from whence his grandfather emigrated to Prince Edward Island in 1829. There, at Lyndale, Donald Lamont was born in 1867.

After a short period of teaching in his native district, he returned to the land of his ancestors to prepare himself for the Christian ministry. Entering the University of Glasgow, he passed through the faculties of Arts and Divinity, his active mind and charming personality long remembered by his student contemporaries.

In 1901 he was ordained to the parish of Waternish, and later translated to the parish of Strath, both in the Isle of Skye. About the beginning of the Great War, he was elected to the parish of North Knapdale, Argylshire; but though his ministry here continued until 1914, it was interrupted by the necessities of war, Mr. Lamont having been called to service as chaplain to British sailors and soldiers in Holland.

Mr. Lamont re-crossed the Atlantic in 1920 to pursue his vocation amongst his friends and kindred in Prince Edward Island. In this charge he remained (with a short interlude in Cape Breton) until his election to Bloor Street Presbyterian Church in Toronto. From Toronto he was called to Dunvegan, and in 1934 he returned to Scotland where he ministered in Mull until his retirement from active work in 1941.

The qualities which drew to Mr. Lamont such a wide circle of friends and admirers—his mental robustness, his delight in adventure, his happy fusion of a steadfast devotion to his calling with a lively sense of the drama and the humour of life–were retained by him to the end.

Well-read in various fields, he was the author of several books having written an account of one of his early parishes *Strath in Isle of Skye*, as well as two volumes of more specifically religious interest, *Seven Great Questions* and *Our Friends After Death*.

Mr. Lamont's wife predeceased him by two years. He leaves one son, James, and one daughter, Margaret, Mrs. MacKenzie, for whom great sympathy will be felt in their loss at this time.

It was while he was in Dervaig that his wife passed away. She was Sarah Lamont, from Rothesay, Scotland, and is buried in Dervaig Cemetery, Mull.

In a letter from Rev. D.M. Lamont to Mr. Aiken of Charlottetown, telling of his wife's death, he writes:

> I must tell in few words what a bright and joyful testimony of her blessed hope, my wife left in her last days and even last hours. This impressed me all the more because her joy was preceded by a period of fear and great darkness. But

the Lord revealed to her His own light and glory. In all her testimony there was not one word of anything she herself did. It was all the Lord—what He did and what He said—what He showed her of his glory.

He is buried in Lambhill Cemetery, near Glasgow Scotland.

Their children were:
C1. James Lamont, married in London, England.
C2. Margaret Lamont, m. 1) James MacKenzie, in Toronto. He was from the Island of Lewis, Scotland. They had issue:
D1. Daughter, died young, buried in Lambhill cemetery, Glasgow, Scotland.
Margaret married 2) Hopkins, in Scotland.

Margaret Anne Lamont

B13. Margaret Anne Lamont, 1870-1903, daughter of Ewen Lamont and Sarah MacPherson, m. Donald Stewart, Caledonia, P.E.I., in Boston, Mass. They came back to P.E.I. to look after his parents, where she died and is buried in Caledonia cemetery. They had one son:
C1. Donald Stewart, died suddenly with a heart attack while serving on the Hamilton, Ontario, Police Force.

Murdoch Lamont, nephew of Malcolm Lamont, the Pioneer

Murdoch was only seven years of age in 1829, therefore it would appear that his parents may not have been living, he seemed to have been treated as a son, by Malcolm, since he and Ewen were left equal shares of the farm, in Lyndale. He must have moved to Stanchel on or about the time of his marriage to Catherine Stewart in 1855, since Ewen seems to have sole possession of Murdock's 50 acres in Lyndale by 1860.

From the website of Karen Linneberg, we find the following information on Murdoch Lamont, nephew of the pioneer Malcolm Lamont. Sources listed were Lamont Family Archives and Fred Dimond.

A1. Murdoch Lamont, 1822-1902, was born in Skye and was a nephew of Malcolm Lamont, the pioneer. He emigrated to P.E.I. with Malcolm and his family in 1829, and eventually settled in Stanchel. In 1855, he married Catherine Stewart, 1834-1914. They had issue:

   B1. Ewen Alexander Lamont, born May 20th, 1856, married on October 1st, 1879, in Springton, P.E.I., Christina MacKinnon, born c. 1860. They had issue:

      C1. Catherine Lamont, born April 26th, 1880.

   B2. Margaret Lamont, born June 19th, 1857, died November 8th, 1946, in Springton, P.E.I.

   B3. Donald Lamont, 1858-1934, m. Christina Anne Matheson, she died in 1932. The had lived in Lot 67 on the Junction Road. They had issue:

      C1. Ewen Lamont, 1888–1959, m. Hilda Cutcliffe, 1907–1980. He was a Cpl in the 26th battalion, CEF, 1914. They had issue:

         D1. Bruce Lamont.

         D2. Iris Lamont.

   B4. Peter Lamont, 1864–1892, lived in Springton, m. Sarah Nicholson.

   B5. Christina Lamont, 1861–1923, married in 1882, in New London, P.E.I., to James Andrew Campbell, 1858–1922, from Graham's Road, P.E.I., with issue:

      C1. Garnett Weldon Campbell, 1882–1949, m. Charlotte Warren, 1883–1956, with issue:

         D1. Vernon J. Campbell.

C2. Robert Campbell, 1884–1893.
C3. James Murdoch Campbell, 1885–1965, m. Margaret J. MacEwen, 1890–1976. They had a family.
C4. Jemima Campbell, 1887–1976, m. Edward B. MacMurdo, 1885–1990.
C5. Catherine Isabella Campbell (Katie), 1888–1961, m. Walford MacEwen, 1888–1984.
C6. Caroline Olive Campbell, 1889–1981, m. Willard Webster Warren, 1881–1925, operated Warren's Mill, before moving to B.C.
C7. John Robert Lamont Campbell, 1892–1959, m. 1) Molly Nora Louise Avison. He m. 2) Florence Strickland (Sherren). He added the name Lamont to his name in later years. A native of Graham's Road, P.E.I., he was a long time contributor to the columns of the *Guardian* under the name "John of the Lilacs." He published a volume of poetry c. 1950. He served for six years in WWI, then went to Regina and Vancouver.
C8. Hugh Archibald Campbell, 1896–1956, buried in New London cemetery. He m. Jessie Catherine MacKay, 1897–1966. He was a long distance runner for three consecutive years. He was a school Superintendent and a church Elder.
B6. Catherine Jane Lamont, 1862–1886, m. David Theodore or Theophillius Mutch, in Strathalbyn.
B7. Isabella Lamont, born April 5th, 1866.
B8. Catherine Margaret Lamont (Cassie), born April 21st, 1868.
B9. Murdoch William Lamont, 1870–1922.
B10. Mary Jane Lamont, 1874–1951, m. John Reddie White. They had a family.

Rev. Donald MacDonald

For a compelling account of the profound effect of the ministry of the Rev. Donald MacDonald, please see Ewen Lamont's *A Biographical Sketch of the Life of the Late Rev. Donald McDonald* at the end of this book.

The Rev. Donald MacDonald emigrated to this country in 1824, spending two years in Cape Breton before coming to Prince Edward Island.

To say that he made a profound impression on many who came under his ministry would be an understatement. The Lamonts, who first settled in upper Vernon River moved to Orwell Head in order to be close to his main preaching station on the east end of the Island.

The Comptons, who were United Empire Loyalists and living in Nova Scotia, left that Province to follow him to Prince Edward Island.

The Hierlihys, the Stymeists, who heard him preach in New Brunswick, forsook all to follow him to the Island and be under his ministry.

Duncan Campbell, author of *The History of Prince Edward Island*, published in 1875, wrote of the Rev. Donald MacDonald:

> In 1826 he came to the Island, and commenced his labours in the spirit of the true evangelist. To him, the toil of travelling over the country and ministering to the destitute was the highest pleasure.
>
> Multitudes flocked to hear him preach. In barns, dwelling-houses, schoolhouses, and in the open air he proclaimed his commission to eager hundreds …
>
> His sermons were masterpieces of logical eloquence. He would begin in a low rather conversational tone; but, as he proceeded, his voice would become stronger. Then the

whole man would preach—tongue, countenance, eyes, feet, hands, body—all would grow eloquent! The audience would unconsciously become magnetized, convicted, and swayed at the speaker's will. Some would cry aloud, some would fall prostrate in terror, while others would clap their hands, or drop down as if dead.

Seldom has such pulpit power been witnessed since the preaching of Wesley, Whitfield, and Edward Irving.

He had rare conversational powers. His spirits were always good. He knew the circumstances of every family in his widely scattered flock, and remembered the names of all the children. He had no certain dwelling-place, no certain stipend, and bestowed all he got on works of charity. His dress, appearance, and manners always bespoke the cultured Christian gentleman …

He had built fourteen churches; he had registered the baptism of two thousand two hundred children, and had baptized perhaps as many more not registered; he had married more people than any living clergyman; he had prayed beside thousands of deathbeds; he had a parish extending from Bedeque to Murray Harbour, and from Rustico to Belle Creek and he had five thousand followers, more attached to their spiritual leader than ever were Highland clansmen to their chief. But he was as humble as a child. To God he gave glory for all.

The [his] funeral was the largest ever witnessed in the colony. All classes united in paying their last tribute of respect to the honoured dead. The cortege numbered over three hundred and fifty sleighs.

As the great procession moved down through the country, at the roadsides and at the doors and windows of the houses might be seen old men weeping, and women and children sobbing as if they had lost a father; and in the presence of a vast assemblage, near the church where his eloquent voice had so often melted listening thousands, and where he had so often celebrated, at the yearly sacrament, the Saviour's death, the remains of the Rev. Donald MacDonald were laid to rest.

Principal Leitch, of Queen's University, Canada, wrote in 1863:

> I had the pleasure of meeting today with the Rev. Donald MacDonald, of whom I had often heard about in Scotland, and whose life forms one of the most singular chapters in the history of Missionary enterprise.
>
> He will take no reward for his labours, except the primitive hospitality of the people. Such disinterested self-sacrifice had a higher reward. The people learned to love and honour him.
>
> His influence has now so widely extended that he has thirteen churches. He makes a circuit among them from Sabbath to Sabbath, and he has elders to conduct devotions when he is not himself present.
>
> The bodily exercises at public worship form a marked peculiarity. The people on account of these exercises, received the opprobrious names of "Jerkers," "Kickers," "Jumpers," etc. Cries of distress (such as "Lord have mercy on me") usually accompany these movements. The people feel, that when wrought into a certain state of mind (deep conviction of sin). They cannot prevent the access of these movements. After a time these give way to another exercise, that of dancing, and clapping of the hands. This is a joyful exercise, expressing the gladness of the sinner when set free from the convictions of sin. When these exercises at first appeared about 30 years ago, he did not know how to interpret them, but as they were accomplished with deep religious feeling, and a change of character, he regarded them as the direct work of the Holy Spirit. With this view of the subject, he felt bound to encourage the work, and in

the course of time it became the most characteristic feature of his form of worship. Sometimes the work comes like a strong tempest and at other periods it subsides into a gentle breeze. It reached its climax shortly after the late revivals in Ireland, but unlike these revivals, it continues in full force. It is not surprising that Mr. MacDonald should at first be perplexed by these psychical phenomena, as he did not enjoy the advantage of those researches which have shed so much light upon the subject.

Mr. MacDonald is saved from any practical error by maintaining the supremacy of the Bible as the rule of life, and by insisting on a walk and conversation becoming the gospel.

The results of his labours is a practical proof of this. His followers are distinguished by the exemplary character of their lives, and are willing to make any sacrifice for the cause of religion.

Mr. MacDonald is now about 80 years of age, but retains the vigour and vivacity of youth. His character in many respects resembles that of Wesley. He is a hearty, hilarious man, with a keen appreciation of the humorous. He has nothing morose or repulsive in his character; but like Wesley, he has a wonderful insight into human nature, and extraordinary tact in governing his own people and advancing their interests. From being an object of reproach and persecution, he is now a personage of great consideration in the community. It is often to him a theme of fervent gratitude that the once despised MacDonald is now courted and honoured as the fit associate of men of high degree. He is, however, humble, and takes none of the glory to himself. He is distinguished by the sternness of his Calvinism and his unswerving loyalty to the Church of Scotland.

In 1939 there was a revival in the churches in the Island of Lewis, Scotland. Rev. Donald Lamont wrote the following letter dated August 4th, 1939:

The Lewis revival (To the Editor of the Stornaway *Gazette*.)

Sir:

If your columns are still open to this arresting subject, may I crave space to relate some experiences of an old minister.

I have been from my youth an eye witness of revivals, both in Scotland and America, of the same type as the present Lewis revival. But I promise to give facts, not opinions. Let the reader consider the facts. Let one especially mention a revival that broke forth among a colony of Gaelic Highlanders in Prince Edward Island, Canada. It was the kind some call hysterical, emotional, fanatical, etc. But when I mention Highlanders I do not imply that we Celts are more prone to exciting frames of religious mind than other races. I have found in America, cool Sassenachs, solid Anglo Yankees and even red Indians just as the Gaels, to weep in the sanctuary when the Spirit was present and to tremble or swoon or leap into ecstasies of joy.

But the first instructive fact I shall mention of the P.E.I. revival is its amazing duration. Not that genuineness of any revival can be judged by its duration. Pentecost was to human eyes short lived: but its results are with us still and the results of every true revival are eternal in Heaven. But God had a purpose in prolonging the P.E.I. movement. For one thing prophecies fathered by a worldly wish became current to the effect that the revival would soon die. It was called a "nine day wonder," a "passing craze," "fits of religion," "mania," etc. But not one of those who spoke thus lived to see the end of it. How long then did it last? If I say twenty years, some will wonder. If I say fifty, some will doubt—but as a matter of history it has now lasted more than a hundred years.

It began under the ministry of Rev. Donald MacDonald of Perthshire, Scotland, as long ago as 1828. MacDonald himself had just emerged from a period of soul distress. He had thought himself doomed to perdition, but was now rejoicing in joy unspeakable and full of glory.

To be brief, the revival began, for henceforth his very voice had in it a supernatural power. Crowds attended his preaching throughout his wide circuits, but not all came to worship. Some came to be amused, standing at the open door of a crowded church. The prayers of the distressed set them into hysterical laughter—but not all. Some came to laugh and remained to pray.

And now let me mention a second fact of this revival for it is instructive. The ruling principle and purpose always and everywhere, was souls seeking refuge in Jesus Christ.

This is clearly true of the Lewis revival but not all revivals are of this type. I have been brought into contact with some avowed spiritual movements of a different sort. I was once asked to a congregation of the Pentecostals (let me not be censorious), but when I talked to the leaders of this church, their highest objective seemed to be the gift of tongues or some sensational miracle of healing. These gifts are good, but our call in P.E.I. was for eternal salvation through Jesus Christ. When Dr. MacLeod of Fiunary, the great Norman, visited our colonial churches in Canada in 1845, he described in his diary his meeting with MacDonald surrounded by a crowd of his followers. MacDonald with his snowy white locks gave Dr. MacLeod a friendly welcome. In testimony of his orthodoxy he raised his voice to say, "I appeal to you, my people, if I have not preached to you the doctrines of the Confession of Faith," which evidences that in his revival, there was no claim to special revelation other than the gospel.

Characteristic of broad-minded Norman was the fact that having been chiefly in company of those who disliked the revival and emphasized the "folly" of its extravagance. He writes, "surely better all this 'folly' with such good results than cold and frigid regularity with no results but death," for he had just mentioned that three thousand people, including fifteen hundred communicants, adhered to MacDonald.

Referring once more to more than one hundred years continuance of P.E.I. revival, a memorable prediction and its remarkable fulfillment will interest readers. MacDonald was too practical a man to pose as a Seer, but when he was an old man approaching eighty, a saying became current, like a proverb, that "when MacDonald dies the revival dies."

He protested publicly against the insinuation that the revival was not of God but of "poor weak MacDonald," as he called himself. It was then he began to tell first his elders and then proclaim publicly that "our churches will be visited with a third revival after I am passed from the earth."

His congregations never forgot this prediction till it was fulfilled in 1890. The strange fulfillment of it is now history. Over twenty years after MacDonald's death a missionary from far off South Sea Island (Rev. John Goodwill) came on a preaching tour of P.E. Island. MacDonald's revival was not then extinct but it was reckoned in a dying condition. Prayer meetings deserted, dance halls crowded. Goodwill had been brought up in Nova Scotia near a colony of Highlanders. He became so interested in them that he acquired their language, Gaelic. I used to listen when a boy with wonder to his English tongue holding forth in eloquent voice. After some years of strenuous toil he saw to his joy the almost sudden breaking forth of what is known as the third revival—a mighty movement that is still alive. The fulfilling of MacDonald's prophecy and now, strange to tell fifty years after this event, his son Rev. Tom Goodwill continues year after year to come to his father's old parish to officiate at great communion gatherings in which the same old ecstasies of revival are present.

Reading today in the Stornaway *Gazette*, the thought struck me how poor old MacDonald, maligned and lonely, would have been cheered by such a Christian God-speed as the Presbytery of Lewis uttered forth so whole-heartedly.

Yours, etc.
D.M. Lamont
Mull, Scotland

A Biographical Sketch of the Late Rev. Donald McDonald
with an appendix

by Ewen Lamont, Elder

Originally published in 1892 by John Coombs, Steam Printer, Queen Street, Charlottetown

Recently, during some casual conversation with different parties, I was asked by some of them whether I could satisfactorily explain the reason why none of the contemporaries of the late Rev. Donald McDonald, or of those who were familiarly acquainted with him since the time he had become celebrated as a revivalist, till his death—why none of them had taken in hand to write a sketch of his life and labours for the information and benefit of those anxious inquirers who never saw him, or heard him preach?

One of those who spoke to me on the subject above alluded to, is a prominent citizen of Charlottetown, whom I have known since the time of his boyhood, and whom I have always found more than ordinarily friendly. He spoke to me very seriously on the subject. He suggested that if any of those who were eye witnesses from first of that remarkable revival which characterized the ministry of Mr. McDonald—if any of them would be considerate enough to transmit it to posterity a written account of it, such a narrative, he believed, would be gladly welcomed by many. He asked me, "Why would I not undertake it?" I said, "That as far as I was concerned, the task appeared to be impossible. That as Mr. McDonald left no autobiography, kept no regular journal, or diary, and as there is nothing in print that would help me, except a few obituary paragraphs, now beyond my reach, I would have to depend chiefly on my memory as a source of supply." "Go on," he said, "and draw upon your memory."

Before parting with my friend, I have a reluctant promise that I would do what I could to satisfy him and others of a like mind. Hence the occasion.

In fulfillment of my promise, I do myself the pleasure of committing the following brief sketch to writing—perhaps to print, at no distant day.

Although I was intimately acquainted with Mr. McDonald for about thirty-six years, yet I never kept a memorandum of his sayings or doings, except in memory.

Perhaps some persons will complain of the obscurity of my statements, as they appear through this medium, as an ancient Celtic bard complained of the obscurity of the traditions of his time, when he sang:

> Cha'n fhaicear ach claon na bh' ann,
> Mar dhearsadh na gealich 'd i faoin,
> Ar linne tha caol 's a ghleann.

> Events of the time that has been
> Are by memory dimly shown;
> As streams in a valley are seen
> By the light of the waning moon.

I inset here the following documents, which will throw some light on what I have taken in hand:

> It is hereby certified that the bearer, the Reverend Donald McDonald, has acted as Missionary Minister, on the Royal Bounty, in Glengarry, a district of the Parish of Kilmanivaig and Presbytery of Abertarff, for the last eight years. That he emigrates to America an unmarried man, and in the full possession of all the privileges of clergyman of the Church of Scotland.
>
> Attested this 24th of June, 1824, by Duncan Macintyre,

minister of Kilmallie; Joseph Cook, J.P.; John Cameron, elder; Alex. Cameron, elder;

That Mr. Donald McDonald, Missionary Minister of Glengarry, within the Parish of Kilmanivaig and Presbytery of Abertaff, was ordained on the second day of August, 1816, a Minister of the Gospel of the Lord Jesus Christ, by the said Presbytery, is attested at the Manse of Boleskine, this 26th day of April, 1825.

William Fraser, Clerk

It is stated in *Campbell's History of P.E. Island*, that he was born on January 1st, 1783. If that be true, he was baptized when four days old.

The following is a copy of the record of his baptism:

Donald, lawful son to Donald McDonald and Christan Stewart, in Drumchastle. Baptized January 4th, 1783. Extracted from the Register of Births and Baptisms of the Parish of Logeirach, on the 6th of August, 1851.

by *Donald Duff*, Clerk

I could related many affecting anecdotes and incidents of his early years, both before and after he was licensed to preach the Gospel, if I were not restricted to relate only what I *know* to be true. I think that I shall be excused if I leave unrecorded what I cannot authenticate.

From Mr. McDonald's early youth the acquirement of knowledge was his ruling passion. He was eager to master the higher branches of learning, but the ministry of the Gospel, at first, had no attraction for him. Worldly pursuits were his aim. Perhaps that was owing to what he overheard his mother say about him at a certain time.

A relative happening to call at his father's house one day

spoke to his mother about him. He said that so promising a boy as her son Donald was, should be encouraged to study for the ministry of the Gospel.

"No," she answered, "I would rather by far to see my Donald follow the occupation of a shepherd; wear his plaid and carry his crook, than to see him strut in the canonicals of a clergyman."

A situation of emolument in the Civil Service of India, was the goal of his ambition, till he became a student of divinity. St. Andrew's University was his Alma Mater. An unsuccessful application for the position above-mentioned, became the turning point of his future course. Then, and not till then, did he decide on studying for the ministry.

I heard him relate all the incidents connected with the unsuccessful application, in detail, but a record of them would take up too much space here.

As far as I know, he never expected to leave his native land to come this side of the Atlantic, until after the untimely and melancholy death of his kind patron, the Chieftain of Glengarry. The sad event happened as follows:

The Chieftain, while on a tour through some of the Hebrides, accompanied by his daughter, had occasion to board a steamboat, which was to call at a certain port, which he intended to visit. As the boat was nearing the quay, he tried to get ashore by jumping off the gunwale of the boat. He jumped off; but instead of gaining a safe footing ashore, he fell head foremost. A sharp stone penetrated his forehead. He was carried to the nearest inn. He called for a mirror. As he gazed at the ugly wound, as reflected by the looking glass, he said as he wiped the streaming blood off his face: "This will not kill a Highlander yet." But the accident proved fatal. The brave Highlander died! Another melancholy circumstance connected with the sad event remains to be narrated. His bereaved daughter accused herself of being the cause of her father's death. While her father was balancing himself for his desperate leap, she attempted to prevent him, by grasping his coat tail. She was too late. Her interference only baffled him. It was the opinion of those who witnessed the sad occurrence, and who knew the strength and agility of the Chieftain, that, if he had not been interfered with, he would have accomplished his daring feat with safety.

In the summer of the year 1824, Mr. McDonald left his native Highlands, never to return. He took his passage in a ship bound for Nova Scotia. He landed at Pictou, but disliking that place he left it and took passage to the Island of Cape Breton. That Island was then a wild place. It was but sparsely settled. Its inhabitants were rude in their manners, and poor in their worldly circumstances. However, it appears that he intended to make it his home for the remainder of his life, for he took up a homestead there. Its locality is still named after him, "*Ruhga mhinisteir*" [The Minister's Point]. He remained in Cape Breton for about two years. I frequently heard him speak about the hardships to which he was exposed while there, in travelling from one settlement to another. He frequently had to travel alone, through trackless forests, with only a pocket compass to guide him. Trudging on snow shoes, Indian fashion; wearing rawhide moccasins; in danger of being torn and devoured by wild beasts. One day as he was thus travelling towards a distant settlement alone, with his pocket compass in hand, he espied a large wild cat right before him, and, as he thought, in the attitude of making a bound at him. He stood, motionless with terror, expecting no other fate than that his mangled body in a few moments would be quivering in the claws and teeth of the savage brute. But, to his unexpected relief, the brute, instead of springing upon him, bounded away, and was soon out of sight. He continued his journey through the woods. As he came in sight of the settlement to which he was going, a partridge crossed his way. He picked up a stick to kill it, but before he had time to smite the poor bird, his conscience smote *him*! "Ungrateful wretch," he said to himself, "kind Providence has just now shielded you from instant death. Is the killing of a harmless creature going to be the first expression of your gratitude?"

From the following strange occurrence, it appears that he had worse enemies to fear than wild beasts.

One night, while travelling to a distant place to which he had been invited, he came to a bridge which spanned a deep and rapid river. Hearing a dog barking behind him, he turned around, and as he did so, the dog passed him, stood between him and the bridge, and would not let him advance another step. The minister then looked at the bridge, and on scanning it closely, noticed that a part of its covering was removed and a gap left open, too wide for any man to step over. That if he had not been obstructed by the dog, he wold inevitably have fallen into the river and been drowned, the night being very dark. The dog, a large, shaggy one, then took hold of one of his coat sleeves, and led him off the main road to a cemetery near the bridge. The dog then let go his grasp, and began to claw and scratch the ground. Then, after uttering a loud whine, he bounded away, and the minister saw him no more. He had many other narrow escapes from death while he remained in Cape Breton, evidencing that his sojourn there was not without its troubles.

As Mr. McDonald left his native Highlands never to return, so he left the Island of Cape Breton, never to return thither. At what time of the year 1826, that he came to this Island, I cannot now exactly say. Neither do I know what were the motives that influenced him to come. Perhaps his strongest inducement was to see his brother Finlay and his family, who then resided at Doctor's River, in King's County, and who afterwards removed to Orwell Head. His brother's family consisted of four sons and six daughters. That family have all passed away except three, two sons and one daughter. One of the surviving sons, Duncan, never married. The youngest, Peter, still occupies the old homestead at Orwell Head. He has, in my judgment, several points of resemblance to the late minister, his uncle.

Mr. McDonald never left this Island while he lived, except on a few solicited visits to the neighbouring Provinces of Nova Scotia and New Brunswick.

There were clear proofs that the people who invited him to visit those Provinces were specially benefited through his ministry there; though he could not spend much of his time with them, on account of the extent of his field of labours on this Island. It was customary for many of them to attend the yearly Communion Services, both at DeSable and Orwell Head, while Mr. McDonald lived.

Whatever were his disappointments and difficulties elsewhere, or whatever were the motives that prompted him to come to this Island, I think it is evident that God overruled them all for his good and the good of others.

The revival under his ministry was in progress when I came to this Island (1830), but I did not see or hear him till the following year (1831). When I first saw him, there was a deep scar in one side of his face, the scarcely healed orifice of a morbid swelling, caused by severe exertions and exposure to cold and wet, before he left Cape Breton.

The sphere of his ministerial labours was then westward of the Hillsborough, but disparaging rumours of him and the revival were afloat in all directions. The strenuous and persistent efforts that were then put forth by his enemies, I still remember as if they were but the events of yesterday. The object of their efforts was to prejudice the public mind against him by every possible means. I have known many, who claimed to be very religious, who would never speak of him except in such contemptible epithets as, "McDonald the jerker," "Kicker McDonald," etc. Those rumours referred to, were as diversified as they were false. To give an idea of their nature, I shall here specify a few: "He is crazy" (the expression then was, "Out of his head"). "Wherever he happens to be a guest for a night, he peremptorily orders the dog, the cat, and the rooster to be killed; asserting that the devil is in them all. He dissuades people from the observance of the Sabbath, maintaining that Saturday is the Bible Sabbath. He is very immoral. Illegitimate children are born to him here and there. Wherever he happens to preach, he puts people out of their head; makes them dance—skip about—tear off their clothes, and play all manner of revolting capers. All such mischief comes from his snuff-box, for he is master of the 'black art.' He was taught it in college. All ministers learn it, but none, except a bad one like him, practises it." Those who were not credulous or superstitious enough to heed such silly reports, would have their prejudices strengthened by other stories, such as: "He is no minister. He was never ordained. He was thrust out of the Church of Scotland, etc."

Threatening rumours would be brought to Mr. McDonald's own ears, also: "He is sure to be waylaid in some sequestered spot and maltreated;" or, "a band of Indians is to fall upon him at night, drag him out of bed and murder him."

Pretended friends would say: "Surely Mr. McDonald should be warned of his danger, and advised to leave the Island." Evidently such rumours left him apprehensive, for he would not travel at that time night or day, alone. And before retiring to bed at night, he would insist on having the outer door barred and bolted.

I am not aware that he was ever personally assaulted, except that on a certain day he met a man on the market square of Charlottetown, who, after belabouring him with much tongue abuse, gave him a violent kick. The minister, in the hearing of all who were present, said: "Sir, will you give me another such kick, this day twelve months?" That man did not live to see the end of another year. I do not relate the above incident from hearsay, I had it from the minister's own mouth.

Once, during the administration of Governor Ready, certain parties lodged a complaint with the Governor against him as a dangerous character. That he was setting people crazy by his terribly vehement harangues, wherever he happened to preach, and that he should be stopped. The Governor told them that Mr. McDonald, a few days previously, laid his credentials before him, which appeared to be valid, and that he must be left in the exercise of his ministerial functions unmolested. Ever after that, he had full immunity from any interference of that kind. Moreover, he was not under the jurisdiction of any Ecclesiastical Court on this Island. If he were, there is little doubt but that he would be summarily dealt with, for the ministers of the Kirk Presbytery of the Island did not, at that time, look with favour on the revival ministry of Mr. McDonald. An old Presbyterian of my acquaintance once told me that, having heard Mr. McDonald preach, and seen the powerful influence by which his hearers were agitated, he asked his pastor whether he could explain to him what caused that work. His pastor replied, "that he believed it to be a kind of epilepsy." "I cannot agree with your reverence," the old main said, "for I have known many who were afflicted with that malady, but I have never heard any of them pray for mercy, or praise the Lord for his redeeming love and grace while under its influence, as I have heard the people do under the influence that manifests itself under Mr. McDonald's preaching." Afterwards, that old man, as long as he lived, was a constant adherent of Mr. McDonald.

The revival was not long in progress when it became a topic of general conversation in town and country. A few learned men of Charlottetown agreed to avail themselves of the first favourable opportunity of hearing him preach, in order to find out whether he preached sound doctrine or not, and whether the work under his ministry was from God or from the devil, for they considered themselves sufficiently enlightened to distinguish truth from error. With that object in view. They attended divine service on the following Sabbath, at the Malpeque Road, a few miles from Charlottetown. As soon as the minister noticed them, he invited them to a seat near where he was standing, as if he understood their object. When the service was over, the minister beckoned to a young female to stand up. She did so. "Now," said he to the men, "you may ask any questions of that young girl concerning her experience." The same girl was powerfully under the work during the services. They asked her many questions, in order to ascertain what was the state of her mind while under the influence which they saw. She answered all their questions clearly, candidly and intelligently, to their full satisfaction. Shortly after the same men interviewed another young man, whom they knew to be the subject of the revival. They asked him whether he knew of anything what would stop that work. "Yes, I do," he answered, "If I join in with any vain, frolicsome company, it will stop; but when I meditate on my condition and pray, I will have it again." Dr. St. Croix, who was one of their number, said: "That work is from God. We must not oppose Mr. McDonald or revile the work which is seen under his ministry."

There was an old widow woman yet living, who was one of the Doctor's servant girls at that time, and who has a clear recollection of the circumstance related above. She says that the Doctor appeared to be a changed man after that. That she often saw him on his knees, wrestling in private prayer. That she never saw him after that with a prayer book before him at his family devotions.

Still, the tongue of detraction, defamation and ridicule, was busily at work against Mr. McDonald and his adherents, and the work under his ministry continued to be mocked. It was often that people would find the roads ahead of them barricaded with stumps and fence poles, when going to, or coming from their places of public worship.

I do not record these things out of any feeling of animosity towards the memory of such anti-revivalists. They now belong to a generation that is past. I mention them to show with what difficulties the minister had to contend, and under what adverse circumstances the revival attained to its permanency.

I mention them to show that the awakening spread and flourished in spite of all the efforts that were put forth to extinguish it. I record them in order to expose the folly of those who would, by contempt and ridicule, hope to cause a man of living faith to relinquish such principles as he believes to be just. Especially when he believes that Heaven seconds his purpose to maintain them. The revival at first progressed but slowly. The first Sacrament that the minister dispensed after his conversion, was dispensed in a private dwelling. The number of conversions was only eleven. Although their number was small, the minister made the encouraging remark, that likely there was no Judas among them, as they were eleven.

There is reason to conclude that the revival began in himself. In other words, he was revived himself first. When he was brought under real conviction, he discontinued preaching. He shunned society as much as he possibly could. He was thought by some to be deranged.

I heard him relate what his experience was at that time. "For seven months," said he, "I was in very great afflictions. The burden of my sins was almost unbearable. I could draw no consolation from the fact that my head was stored with literary knowledge, and that I was a preacher for many years. It was rather an aggravation of my misery. Fully convinced that my condition in the past was that of a man dead in sins and trespasses; a child of wrath; under the curse of the broken law; obnoxious to all the punishment due on account of my sins—liable to all the miseries of this life, to death itself, and to the pains of hell forever. I strove for relief in various ways, but I found all my efforts as futile as those of a condemned criminal in prison, clanking the chains which he cannot break. One day, being at my wits' ends, I withdrew to my bedroom, and fell on my knees. But I had no utterance in prayer. My head seemed to be as dry as a piece of cork. But thanks be to God, I was relieved. My bands were burst asunder. My soul was brought out of prison. Old things were passed away, and all things were become new. I was filled with all joy and peace in believing. My closed lips were opened, and I spoke aloud in these words: THE UNBOUNDED MERCY OF GOD, AND ALL THE SUFFICIENCY OF THE LORD JESUS CHRIST. My head became a fountain, and tears of joy flowed from mine eyes in copious streams. My host heard me. He came in and asked me in anger, 'Are you beside yourself?'"

HIS PERSONAL APPEARANCE. HIS MANNER OF PREACHING, AND THE APPARENT EFFECT OF HIS PREACHING ON THE AUDIENCE.

Ere I attempts a delineation of the above, I must unroll anew the volume of my memory.

Now, suppose it is a fine summer morning in the year 1832, and that you and I, reader, decide to go and see Mr. McDonald, and hear him preach. We make an early start, as we have several miles to travel. We are joined by others as we walk along. We see others coming to the main road from lanes and bypaths. Look at that barn yonder, with some people standing in front of it, and some others squatted on the grass near it. Mr. McDonald is to preach there today!

We are now at the barn. Let us go in. Now, let us climb this ladder to the loft before the place gets too crowded. We notice that the seats are but boards and planks laid over blocks of wood. Many of the seats are already occupied. Do you see that empty chair near the back door? It is the pulpit. The young men sitting on both sides of it are young converts; ruling elders of future congregations. There is a crowd coming up from the gate. The man that you see walking leisurely in front, wearing a black suit and a beaver hat, is the minister. He comes in and occupies the chair. There is now a rush for the seats, until the place is crowded to its utmost capacity. The lofts are now crowded with young boys, and every one of them appearing to be thoughtful and serious. Since you never saw Mr. McDonald, you are bound to scrutinize his looks and motions. You conjecture his age to be between forty-five and fifty years. You notice that his stature is below average, but that he is uncommonly stout in body. His head is large. His hair, which he wears short, is sprinkled over with grey. His forehead high, broad and massive. His eyes, deep set, and of a hazely colour, and full of expressiveness. His nose long and aquiline. His cheeks pale, but slightly tinged with red. His mouth small, his lips compressed. His chin short and pointed. His neck short and stout. His hands small and white. If you would describe his looks in one word, that word would be, *careworn*!

The Rev. Donald MacDonald
Mr. MacDonald never permitted himself to be photographed. This sketch was drawn from life by John McKinnon of Uigg and retouched by several photographers.

See! He is about to begin the service. First, he directs the young converts to sing a few, short evangelical hymns, and cautions them to avoid a low, listless, drawling manner. You notice that every one in the audience that *can*, sings. As soon as the singing begins, the audience becomes visibly affected. You hear the clapping of hands here and there among the people. You hear expressions of mental distress and sorrow; and some of joy and gladness; and you cannot tell which of the two kinds predominates. You hear some of the young boys occupying the lofts, utter piercing cries, as if shot.

The minister now stands on the chair, takes a pinch of snuff, puts on his spectacles, reads a Psalm and sings a few stanzas, he himself leading as precentor. Then he offers his opening prayer, remarkable for its fervency and childlike simplicity. When his opening prayer is ended, he orders all the stricken ones among those occupying the lofts to be taken down and placed near himself. Before his announces his text, he comments on the responsibility of his position as a messenger of Christ, and warns his hearers against the danger of slighting his message. His text is, "Cursed is every one that continueth not in all things which are written in the book of the law to do them."—Gal. 3:10. He begins in a conversational manner. The expression of his face is calm. There is no attempt at oratory. No written notes. No theatrical gestures. No furtive glances at a manuscript sermon. He quotes nothing from uninspired authors in support of his views. His quotations are from the Bible only. As he enters more deeply into the theme of his discourse, his countenance becomes flushed and animated. His utterances increase in force and pathos. The tone of his voice now becomes loud and solemn, almost as monotonous as the sound of a mountain torrent His voice is never tremulous; never rises into shrillness, or drops into a whisper. His whole body is in motion, as if thrilled through and through by the extreme energy of his mind. He holds a napkin in his hands, folding and unfolding it, as if unconscious of what his hands are doing. Now and then he takes the napkin in one hand and wipes his face and neck with it, till it gets too wet to be used. Now you see the sweat commingle with his tears, and run in streams over his face; and you can see that the collar and bosom of his shirt are wet as if taken out of the wash tub. Now the sermon is ended. He reads a Psalm, and sings a few stanzas as before, offers his concluding prayer, and pronounces the benediction.

Having heard the discourse, can we epitomize it? We might give the words of it, but not the life and energy with which it was delivered. He began by dilating on the woeful misery incurred by man for time and eternity, by the breaking and dishonouring of the law of God. Then he enlarged on the inexorability of the law. Then, on man's utter inability to satisfy the demands of the law. He showed that the law demanded full and complete satisfaction in all its points, and cried for vengeance upon its transgressors. That man, stripped of his original righteousness and swayed by the carnal mind, which is enmity against God, could never yield perfect obedience to the law; which is spiritual, just, holy and good. He then spoke of the covenant of grace, its ample provisions, and its suitableness to fallen man, in all his exigencies. Spoke of Christ as its surety, and that He, by His vicarious sufferings and death on the cross, purchased not only eternal redemption, but also an eternal inheritance in the regions of glory for all who would accept of Him, as he is freely offered in the Gospel. He then concluded by an earnest call to sinners to turn from their evil way, and from the evil of their doings, and to flee from the wrath to come, by coming to Christ as the only refuge for sinners.

The people are in no hurry to dismiss. You hear sobs and cries among them. Some run out, as in a fright; others are standing at the door, with grinning, mocking faces, and some are standing outside, laughing. But the people inside show no inclination to leave. Some are crying earnestly for mercy. Some are leaping and praising God, with a loud voice in the ecstasy of spiritual joy. The services are further protracted. The minister calls on some of the elders to lead in prayer, then to sing some hymns. You know that the minister approves of those extraordinary movements by his quoting of some countenancing passages of Scripture, such as: "Then shall the virgin rejoice in the dance, both young men and old together." "All people clap your hands to God." "There was a noise, and behold a shaking." "Ask ye now and see whether a man doth travail with child? Wherefore do I see every man with his hands on his loins as a woman in travail, and all faces are turned into paleness?" etc.

Now, as the people are leaving, let us retrace our steps. As we return, we notice that the young folks are forming themselves in groups and bands, and singing as they go to their respective places of abode.

It was predicted by many that the revival would dwindle away and become extinct, before the end of three years. But finding that at the end of that time the work was still spreading and strengthening. They began to modify their prediction, by admitting that it might continue during the term of Mr. McDonald's natural life, but no longer.

Shortly after his conversion, a delegation waited on him from a district of this Island, inhabited by Presbyterians, with the offer of a fair stipend, if he would consent to become their pastor. He asked permission to withdraw for a short time to consider their proposal, as it was an important one. When alone, the following mandatory words in Gaelic were indelibly impressed on his mind. "*Tha thu saor—fuirich saor*" [You are free—remain free]. He then presented himself before the delegation, and said: "I am free and I shall remain free." He acted on that determination while he lived.

I happened to be present when a man asked him how much was his yearly stipend. The minister's reply was: "If you will tell me how much was the Apostle Paul's, I will tell you the amount of mine." He detested the idea of looking on the preaching of the Gospel as a money-making business. He chiefly depended on the free-will offerings of his people for his maintenance. The manner of ascertaining the amount of the offerings so given, was as follows: In every meeting or preaching station, an elder would be appointed to keep a record or list of the contributions of every individual. Then on the Monday following the communion service, those lists would be added up, and handed to the minister. He would read publicly the amount of every list (but not the names of individuals) and their sum total. Then, occasionally, he would pass some remarks on the amount received: "If you consider the sum too small for me, add to it; if too much, take it from me. I receive just what my Master sees fit for me. No more, no less."

If anyone would venture on measuring lances with him in religious controversy, that man would meet with such treatment as would make him repent of his temerity. He had no toleration for religious hypocrites. He would make quick work of getting rid of infidels and sceptics. A sceptic who happened to hear him preach, asked him at the close of the service: "Who is that mythical being that you called the devil?" The minister acted at first as if he did not hear him. He fumbled for his snuff-box and took an ample pinch. He then looked the men straight in the face, and with an ominous frown, and in a voice of thunder said: "YOUR FATHER, SIR!" The man looked as if bewildered. But soon collecting his scattered wits, he boldly faced the minister, and challenged him to a public discussion. The minister, pointing to the Bible, said, "I will meet you there, Sir, and nowhere else."

HIS FIRST PASTORAL VISIT TO THE MURRAY HARBOUR CHURCH

Previous to the years 1829, 1830, both sides of the Murray Harbour Road to the shore settlements, were but wild woods, uninhabited except by a few families, who emigrated from Scotland in the year 1821. In the years first above-named, many emigrants from the Highlands and the Islands of Scotland, chiefly from Skye, made choice of the lands bordering on the

Murray Harbour Road, as their future homes, to the number of about ninety families, for a distance of about six miles; a large settlement, comprising within its limits the several localities now named Uigg, Kinross, Lyndale, and Grandview. As far as I am aware. They had no capital beginning, except their brave willing hearts and strong limbs. By the assistance and example of their friends and fellow colonists occupying the shore settlements since the year 1803. They soon learned to fell and chop trees, and build their own dwellings. Thus, in a short time, all the immigrants were provided with dwelling houses of their own. These houses were but small, round log huts, roofed with slabs, or the bark of trees, with the seams between the logs tightly caulked with moss. A few hands would build one of them in two or three days. The course of the main road itself could be easily known, the trees in its line being conspicuously "blazed," and windfalls and brush removed, in order to make sleighing in winter possible.

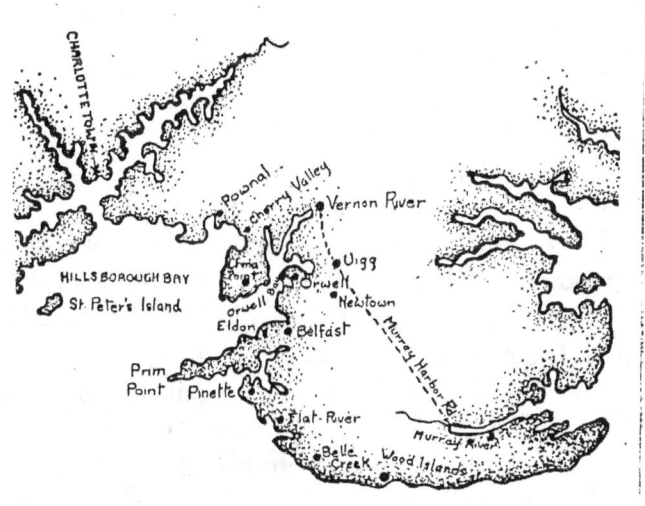

These people were brought up at home under the ministry of the Word, in the enjoyment of Gospel ordinances, and receiving Church privileges. Some of the old people could read their Gaelic Bibles, and the most of their young folks were well versed in Gaelic literature. But in spite of their advantages, and in spite of their claim to morality and religion, the superstition of bygone days tainted the minds of many of them. Some of them firmly believed in the existence of fairies. They believed that the power of wizards and witches to do mischief, far exceeded common belief. They believed that they could, if they chose, by the performance of some mysterious rites, and by the reciting of some incantatory rhymes, known only to themselves, abstract from some milch cows all the virtue of their milk, and enrich the milk of other cows by the same.

The Murray Harbour Road thus colonized, contained about 450 of a population within its vicinity, without any place of public worship, or regular gospel ministry. But they were not altogether destitute. One of their number, a man of acknowledged piety, a good Gaelic, English, and Latin scholar, used occasionally to conduct public prayer meetings for their edification. Such was the condition of the people referred to, and such was their position when the fame of Mr. McDonald reached their ears.

The revival under his ministry then extended eastward, as far as Birch Hill, Lot 49, distant from the Murray Harbour Road Settlement twelve or fourteen miles. Some of their youth of both sexes went there to hear him preach. Some of them were awakened under his preaching. They came back under "*McDonald's work*," as the revival was then misnamed by its enemies. The news of that fact spread like fire through the settlement. The old people, heads of families, were aroused. They must search further into the matter. They must ascertain whether Mr. McDonald is a true minister of Christ, or is he in league with *Moisean* to lead people into a state of fatuity and fascination. They deemed the question to be of too much importance to be indifferent about it. In their dilemma they thought of the man who used to conduct their prayer meetings in his own dwelling. They called on him and earnestly entreated that he would go and hear Mr. McDonald preach, and then let them know his opinion of him, and of the work that accompanied his ministry. When he consented to comply with their request. They cautioned him, at his peril, not to partake of Mr. McDonald's snuff! He solemnly promised that would not touch his *Bucas*, or partake of *any of its contents*. He started for Birch Hill, early on the morning of the following Sabbath. He arrived at the place of meeting, a private dwelling, a while before the services of the day began. The minister was conversing outside with a crowd of people who came to hear him preach. The man stood at a little distance off, as he was a stranger to them all. He was of a prepossessing appearance; then in the prime of his manhood, wearing a plaid of the tartan of his clan. The minister, attracted by the striking mien of the Highlander, walked over to where he stood, spoke to him in Gaelic, and as a further token of welcome and cordiality, handed him the well filled *Bucas*. The man took a pinch between his fingers, but, mindful of his solemn promise, instead of inhaling it into his nostrils, he let it drop out of his fingers unobserved by the minister. He heard the minister preach, and remained till all the services of the day were over. After his return he declared in the presence of those who sent him, that, although he heard many a sermon, he never before heard the Gospel preached in such perspicuity of language, nor with such thorough earnestness and apparent good effect, as he heard it preached at Birch Hill, last Sabbath, by Mr. McDonald. As for the snuff story, he declared it to be simply a device for the devil to prejudice the minds of the people, to their own hurt, against a true messenger of Christ. That man was subsequently ordained into the eldership by Mr. McDonald. He over lived him by many years, and was a hundred years old when he died.

To return to my narrative. The man's words caused a revulsion of feeling in favour of the minister. On the Sabbath following, many of the people, old and young, went to hear him. Some were awakened. When parting with the minister. They asked him if they might expect a visit from him at their own settlement? He readily consented, and asked if they could prepare a suitable place of meeting, where he could preach next Sabbath? One of the men answered, "that, as their dwelling houses were but small, he could not think of a more suitable place than a barn; and as his was as suitable as any other in the settlement, he would freely give it." He told them "that God willing, he would be at their settlement next Saturday." Some of the people went to meet him on his way coming. When he saw them he was overcome with a feeling of compassion, and cried, with tears: "*Sheep* WITHOUT A SHEPHERD." Word was sent through the settlement that he was to preach in such a man's barn, on the Sabbath following. On Sabbath morning some timorous parties met at a neighbour's house to decide whether it was safe to hear Mr. McDonald preach. The good man of the house volunteered to attend the morning service as judge. The rest agreed to await his return. He came back and reported favourably. He said that he was much annoyed by the tantrums of a young woman that kept on continually clapping her hands and dancing. That sometimes she would drown the minister's voice by her loud speaking. He then stepped on the floor and began to imitate her by clapping his hands and dancing. In doing so, he struck his head against one of the loft beams. He put his hand to his head. He looked at his hand. It was covered with blood. "JUDGMENT!" he cried. One of the women present offered to tie a napkin around his head. "No!" he said, "Let the guilty head bleed." That man also was after one of Mr. McDonald's elders. He survived him several years, and died in his ninetieth year. The minister preached on that day with great acceptance and manifest effect. The Presbyterians became greatly attached to him, and he to them, with the exception of a few who made themselves odious by their gainsaying and mocking.

The Murray Harbour settlement soon afterwards became

one of Mr. McDonald's preaching stations. Many of its people professed to have come to the knowledge of the truth, as it is in Jesus, through his instrumentality. Many of them were brought under conviction of sin; and some of them professed to be filled with all joy and peace in believing. After a few of his pastoral visits, none of their barns or dwelling houses could accommodate the large crowds that were flocking to hear him. They soon found it necessary to build a meeting house. Their first Church building cost them nothing beyond their own labour, except a small outlay for nails and windows. It was built of large hemlock trees, that stood in sufficient numbers near its selected site, and hewn to the proper size. Its roof was covered with pine shingles. The crevices in the wall were tightly caulked with moss. The crevices thus caulked, used to be a source of disturbance to the worshippers within, especially at the times of communion, affording to outside mockers a chance to thrust sharp pointed sticks through the moss caulking to the annoyance and bodily injury of those sitting close to the walls within. There are some people yet living who may recollect how they used to be pestered in the same way, when worshipping in houses similarly constructed. However, that building served its purpose for a period of ten years, after which a larger and more comfortable house was erected. It also suited its purpose for a further period of twenty years; at the end of which time the present Church building was erected, being the year 1862. The minister dispensed the Sacrament in it for the first time in the eightieth year of his life.

Of all his regular preaching stations on this side of the Hillsborough, namely those on Lots 48 and 49, and those at the Murray Harbour Road, Point Prim, Belle Creek, Murray River, and Brooklyn, that at the Murray Harbour Road was the most central and populous. It was looked to by the people of the other stations as their headquarters; being the place where they used to partake, yearly, of the elements of the Lord's Supper, under the ministry of Mr. McDonald.

In the summer of 1861, a remarkable religious movement affected the young people of the several preaching stations of Mr. McDonald almost simultaneously. Scarcely a corner of his extensive field of labours remained uninfluenced. Likewise many of the old people who were subjects of the awakening that began over thirty years before, publicly declared that they were benefited afresh by its inspiring flatus. I have known young children, down to nine years of age, to be visibly affected. So conspicuous was it in its manifestations, that it became the subject of several articles of comment in the public newspapers. It was a surprise to many, and was not expected by any. The minister named it *The second revival*; and predicted that there would be a *Third revival*, "but," said he, "who of us will live to witness it?"

None appeared to be so much astonished as those who attributed the work that was to be seen under Mr. McDonald's ministry to his personal magnetism. For they well knew that he was then bordering on his eightieth year, and that bodily infirmities and loss of memory were gaining rapidly upon him.

The sphere of his ministry continued to extend, and the number of his adherents to increase, until he became incapacitated, by old age and bodily infirmities, to minister to their spiritual necessities.

Orwell Head and DeSable were his central preaching stations, where he used to dispense, yearly, the elements of the Lord's Supper to many hundreds of communicants. He composed and published many hymns in English and Gaelic. He was equally at home in both languages. He published a Treatise on the Millennium, another on Baptism; a third on the Plan of Salvation, unfinished, as found in manuscript, among his papers, and published after his death. He was never married; never had a home of his own. He lived with his people and for his people, ever a welcome guest. Always taking a lively interest in their prosperity, and sympathizing with them in adversity. Ever ready to assist the poor and needy, irrespective of their creed or nationality.

After a few weeks' illness, he died at Southport, on the 22nd February, 1867, in the 85th year of his age; trusting in the merits of the Redeemer. His remains were interred in the Orwell Head cemetery, where a monument is erected to his memory, bearing suitable inscriptions in Greek, Latin, English and Gaelic.

Appendix to the Foregoing Sketch

Ewen Lamont in 1892, the year the
Appendix was written

As a period of over twenty-five years has now elapsed since the death of the man whose life and labours I have been reviewing in the foregoing sketch, I suppose the reader would expect me to mention the changes, if any, that have taken place, up to the present time, in the religious condition of the people over whom his ministry exerted such controlling influence. Let the reader peruse what follows.

When it became evident that Mr. McDonald was getting to be unfit for the active work of the ministry, on account of his old age and his daily increasing infirmities, speculation was rife as to what would likely befall his people after his decease, which, according to the course of nature, could not far off. Would they hold their standing as a distinct Christian sect, or cast in their lots with other Presbyterians? was a question frequently discussed both by themselves and by others not belonging to their religious society.

At the time referred to in the above paragraph, a man who paid him a friendly visit, asked him what rules did he prescribe for his people, and in whose charge was he going to leave them when they would be deprived of his ministry? "I direct and charge them to follow the rules and precepts of the Gospel: and I commit them to the care of Christ, the good Shepherd, who gave his life for the sheep," was his prompt answer.

Another minister of the Established Church of Scotland, who called to see him, spoke to him of the dangers to which his people would likely be exposed in the event of their not being subjected to the immediate, direct and active control of the Church before his death. "I compare you and your people," said he, "to a string of beads. When the string is broken, the beads are scattered in all directions!" He received the following reply: "Well, then, when the string is broken, you look after the beads."

While Mr. McDonald lived, his adherents were visibly united as one ecclesiastical body, guided by the same rules, professing the same belief, yearly sitting at the same Communion Table, no matter how far they might be apart as to their different localities. I think it is right for me here to mention their numerical strength and social importance at the time of Mr. McDonald's death. From their small number of eleven, as at their first Sacrament. They increased to the number of many thousands. From the insignificantly small sect slurringly called "Jerkers," "Kickers," etc.. They became a large, influential, and respected body of people, who could, by their united votes, either sustain or upset a Government. Moreover. They would be more than welcome to join any branch of the Presbyterian Church. But after his death changes came and divisions arose, as might be easily foreseen.

Pursuant to public notices, two consecutive public meetings of elders and other male adherents were held. The first at DeSable, the second at Orwell Head, to deliberate and decide upon the best possible means of supplying the vacancy caused by the death of their late lamented leader. Previously their ecclesiastical affairs used to be conducted by the elders, constituted as a Presbytery, over which their late minister, as moderator, held great sway. In him they placed their unbounded confidence. They would ever follow his directions with unanimous alacrity. But now the case is different. The elders meet to deliberate upon a question of much more importance than any question ever brought before them. The one who used to preside with so much ability and acceptance is absent when his presence appears to be most needed.

In giving a cursory, retrospective glance over the transactions of those two meetings, if I am obliged to light upon some things that bring a feeling of sadness upon me; it is with pleasure that I am enabled to state, that, at no time, did their discussions degenerate into angry disputations. Every one that spoke received a patient and respectful hearing. Indeed, all were urgently entreated to give public expression to their thoughts upon the question that was then under their deliberations. But when a considerable number of the elders had spoken, it was painfully evident that they did not see eye to eye, and that their wonted unanimity was about to encounter a violent shock.

When we bear in mind that the Christian Church, even in apostolic times, was frequently disturbed and perplexed by disputes and divisions, need we wonder if the like would now occur? When we reflect upon the fact, that such eminent apostolic men as Paul and Barnabas disagreed about whom to choose as their minister, and that the contention was so sharp between them that they departed asunder one from the other about that question: need we think it strange that the elders and brethren at those meetings could not unanimously agree upon whom to call upon to fill the vacancy above referred to?

At the DeSable meeting an elder, while expressing his views, complained of undue haste and informalities in calling the meeting. Another said in reply that no harm could possibly follow, as the proceedings of the meeting could be considered as only preliminary, and the questions mooted left open for the discussion and final decision of another public meeting to be held at Orwell Head, sure to be held in due time and order. Some counselled delay, and to wait patiently until the chief Shepherd would send them a supply for their spiritual wants in His own good time and way. But others would not consent to a suspension of the ministry of Gospel ordinances, fearing that their people might seek them at the hands of men of other denominations. A majority of the elders present spoke in favour of accepting the services of friendly Kirk ministers until a successor to their late minister would be appointed in accordance with that clause in his will which says that he must be a "duly qualified and recognized member of the Established Church of Scotland." Here a sharp contention ensued about the phrase "duly qualified." How was it to be truly defined in this case? Then an elder spoke to this effect: If that clause recognizes the appointment of a man devoid of the spirit of Christ, having merely the form of godliness but denying its power, though otherwise qualified and recognized as a Kirk minister, I for one would not hesitate to reject the ministry of that man; and moreover, I would not hesitate to disregard that clause. And further, I contend that the phrase "duly qualified" in that clause, never recognizes the absence of spiritual qualification. I believe that the spirit of that clause demands that our late minister's successor shall be a converted man; fitted by the grace of God to nourish and feed the flock; endued with power from on high. After a pause which lasted a considerable time, another elder said that, although he agreed in sentiment with the last speaker, and though he was prepared to act under like circumstances just as he said he would act, and though he freely admitted that there were ministers in the Kirk unworthy of her bread, and unworthy of the name they bear, yet, he rejoiced in the belief that there are men even within her pale that would stand the test of the standard of qualification insisted upon by the last speaker. He was cheered as he sat down. But a respectable minority of the elders present expressed their dissent from the proposition of the majority. Several of them spoke, one after another, to the following effect: That although Mr. McDonald discharged his ministerial functions in virtue of his being licentiated and ordained in the Church of Scotland. Though he never disavowed her doctrines as epitomized in her Shorter Catechism; though he never intended to alienate himself from her; yet when a work begun under his ministry which work was not only slighted but publicly denounced by the Island Kirk ministers of that time as a delusion, it was then that he found that if would continue to own them as brethren he would also have to repudiate and condemn that work. They withdrew from *him* and he from *them*. Thenceforward he was free, and he left us free. Now we fear that such men as they were may come in among us, through a misconstruction of the clause aforenamed, to discountenance and ridicule the work that is yet seen among us, and to entangle us with the yoke of bondage. Some may come in privily to spy out our liberty. Let us beware! Let us remember the warnings of our late minister, earnestly and solemnly sounded in our ears, at more than one sacramental gathering: "Elders, learn! learn!! You do not know how soon you may have to perform these duties yourselves. Never! never!! allow an unconverted minister to stand at the head of this table." In conclusion they quoted several passages of Scripture in proof of the authority of elders to labour in the word and doctrine.

Their deliberations were brought to a close at the meeting

which was subsequently held at Orwell Head. No new topic was brought forward. The question discussed at DeSable and here was put to a vote. The right to vote was vested in two elders from every meeting or preaching station on both sides of the Hillsborough. Twenty-one elders voted. Fourteen in favour of the views of the majority. Seven in favour of those of the minority. No compromise. Thus the die was cast. Formerly they were visibly one. Now they are split into two parties, with this peculiar exception, that some would occasionally sever their connection with the minority and join the majority. And *conversely*, others would sever their connection with the majority and join the minority. Is there not an invisible bond of union uniting all true Christians of every sect and denomination, one to another and to their invisible Head, that all the powers of darkness cannot sever? A Paul and a Barnabas may quarrel and separate. Will that sever the bond of their spiritual union?

The minority after a long but unavoidable delay, appointed some of their elders to the lead, and to dispense the ordinances of the Gospel. But after a time, the spirit of discord troubled them. They disagreed and split. They became two parties; and so continue to this day.

The majority likewise had their troubles. They too disagreed and split, and became two parties, though under somewhat different circumstance, and so continue to this day, as will be shown hereafter.

The first regular ministry employed after Mr. McDonald's death, by the majority, was that of the Rev. James McColl, who, like the writer of this sketch, was more at home in Gaelic than in English. He resigned his charge after a few years' service. He left the Island in answer to a "call" from a Nova Scotian congregation. After remaining there for a short time he emigrated with his family to his native Highlands. By the retirement of Mr. McColl, the field in which he laboured again became vacant. In the summer of 1874, a call from the people interested in this matter on this side of the Hillsborough, was sent to the Rev. Mr. Goodwill, then on his way home from one of the South Sea Islands, where he spent five or six years as missionary from the Kirk in the Lower Provinces to the heathen. In the summer aforesaid, the ministers of both branches of the Church of Scotland on this Island (Free and Established) together with their congregations, joined the United Presbyterian Church of the Dominion of Canada. But the "MacDonaldites," so named by some, stood aloof. They were a large body of people then without a minister. They never objected to the name given them in public print: "*Church of Scotland unattached.*" What were they going to do? Were not many of their leading men known to be in favour of uniting with the new Presbyterian Church? Should they not be cordially invited? No time should be lost. The Rev. Mr. Goodwill was known then to be on his way to the Island. If he would find the "MacDonaldites" in the Presbyterian Union on his arrival, he would be likely to follow suit.

Soon a movement was made in the direction indicated. A meeting was publicly announced to be held on such day in the Orwell Head Church, to consider the question of "Union." The meeting was accordingly held and numerously attended. Three "Union" ministers were present: The Revds. Mr. Melville, of Georgetown; Mr. McLean, of Belfast; and Mr. McLeod, of Charlottetown. After these ministers had expatiated with glowing eloquence on the bright prospects before the United Presbyterian Church of the Dominion of Canada, a Resolution was placed in the hands of the chairman, which, if submitted and passed, would decide the question in favour of Union. But there were so many angry expressions of decided opposition to it, that none would make a motion in favour of it. When another Resolution to counteract it was called for, a man stood up and cried excitedly: "We want no Resolution. Let us alone!" So the question was dropped, and the meeting brought to a close.

Mr. Goodwill shortly after came to Orwell Head. He

preached there on the first Sabbath after his arrival. A meeting was announced to be held in the Church on the following Monday to ascertain the result of the "call." The meeting was duly held. Mr. Goodwill was present. Two elders from the west were present also. When the meeting was duly constituted and declared ready for business, Mr. Goodwill standing in the pulpit, spoke to this effect: I have heard of the "call" you sent me, though I never saw it. I do not wish to see it. I cannot comply with its conditions, for I have found out that they would confine my ministerial work to this side of the Hillsborough. Are there not people on the other side equally in need of my services? Here an elder from the west spoke and said that he and his brother elder were sent to solicit for the DeSable Parish a share of Mr. Goodwill's ministry. The minister said that (D.V.) their request would be granted. A voice to Mr. Goodwill, "What about your stipend!" He replied, "That's your business, and not mine." Another voice, "What are DeSable people to us?" Then another voice, "Humph! The DeSable people want but a share now; by and by. They will take all." One of the elders from the west, Mr. John Bell, referring to the minister's stipend, said that he had no fear but that the people concerned would provide a stipend as fair as that of any minister on the Island. Two Resolutions were passed by small majorities. One in favour of DeSable Parish being included within the sphere of the minister's pastoral labours. The other in favour of leaving their present subscription lists for the minister's stipend undiminished as to their amount. The meeting was closed, and the elders from the west left for their homes, thankful for the success of their mission.

A few words in reference to the dropped "call." To it was attached a legal bond, guaranteeing a stipend of $800 and a free parsonage. The writer was one of its sureties. When the stipend lists were received and their sums added up. They would found to be short by $200. How was the deficiency to be supplied? Easily. Announce a picnic. Call the rowdies.

Furnish plenty of beer with, perhaps, a "stick" in it to make them lavish. Bring the cakes and sell them, slice by slice, at fancy prices. Erect the drinking booth and the dancing stage. Put up the swing, though to the danger of life and limb. What of that? Prepare the "tug of war," where energy of brain is at a discount, but where energy of brawn is at a premium; so that money may come in for the cause of Christ; that godliness may be cherished and promoted in the land. Does not the end justify the means? *Ochoin, Ochoin!*

I should mention in justice to Mr. Goodwill, that no portion of his salary was raised in that questionable manner, either here or elsewhere. I am mistaken in the man if he would take it, if procured in that way. For about eleven years Mr. Goodwill continued his arduous labours, having the Orwell Head congregation within the bounds of his field of work. But a split was about to take place between that congregation and the people of DeSable Parish, and no man was found able to prevent it. The people of that Parish, having learned that the Orwell Head people were preparing to sever connection with them and join in another Church. They sent over nine of their prominent men, the most if not all of them elders, in order if possible to dissuade them; but all to no purpose or avail. A split followed. The Orwell Head Church was incorporated in the year 1883. Mr. Goodwill dispensed the elements of the Lord's Supper in it for the last time in July, the twelfth day, 1885. It was received into the United Presbyterian Church of the Dominion of Canada, in the year 1886.

It must not be inferred from the above that the Orwell Head Parish as a whole entered the "Union." All the other stations over which the late Mr. McDonald presided on this side of the Hillsborough disapproved of the move and kept aloof, as well as many of the people of the Orwell Head congregation itself. That is why Mr. Goodwill holds yearly Communion Services at Birch Hill. And that is why the Orwell Head congregation found it necessary to join with a section of the Belfast Parish, for without doing so. They would be a self-sustaining congregation. They would be too weak to make the minimum stipend up, which is required by the Union Church for her ministers.

To the record of such events as I have noticed, and of which I was the eye witness, and a close observer in the past, I have the following to add. And I plead with the reader to ponder it, because the transaction to which I solicit attention has been misrepresented by some as a shameful proceeding, and by others as a disgraceful row.

At Brooklyn, in July last, on the Saturday before the Communion Sabbath, while the elders were in session, as is usual on such occasions, some grave charges were brought before them, by men of unquestionable veracity, against some intending communicants present, namely: That those arraigned, maintained and taught that no portion of the human race was to be consigned to eternal misery, let them be ever so wicked in this world. That no person need fear hell as a place of endless torment. That even Judas Iscariot is not lost. That the wheat in the parable represents all mankind, and that the tares represent no part or portion whatever of the human race. The whole proceeding took place publicly before the whole assembly. As the arraigned denied none of the charges preferred, and as they would not acknowledge their views to be wrong. They were suspended from Church fellowship, until they would publicly renounce their heresy.

May the example set by the Brooklyn Session cease not to be followed wherever it is needed, until heresy be no more!

In the foregoing "Sketch" and "Appendix," I have briefly recorded some incidents of the past, as they were imprinted long ago on my memory, concerning that notable revival of religion that began over sixty years ago on this Island under the ministry of the late Rev. Donald McDonald, of which I was a subject, and to which I was an eye witness. Now in my old age, it is my happy lot to be an eye witness to another remarkable revival, began a few months ago, under the ministry of the Rev. John Goodwill, and which I believe to be essentially the same as the other two revivals referred to in my "Sketch," if not more powerful in its influence and more rapid in its progress; many hundreds, old and young, and of different nationalities and sects being affected already by it. I would advise any person who, when comparing the characteristics of past revivals with these of the present, finds a disparity in some things, to ponder the following passage of Scripture: "Now there are diversities of gifts, but the same Spirit. And there are differences of administrations, but the same Lord. And there are diversities of operations, but it is the same God who worketh in all."—I Cor. 12:4-6.

We know that wheresoever and whensoever genuine revivals take place, the enemy will try to counteract their influence, for he knows that God by their means delivers many a precious soul from the power of darkness and translates them into the kingdom of His dear Son.

A person purposely witnessing this revival, and going away without being convinced of its reality, is, in my opinion, lacking in spiritual discernment, having eyes that do not see, ears that do not hear, and a heart that does not understand.

Slan leibh, 'n latha chi's nach fhaic.

Ewen Lamont, Elder
Lyndale, P.E.I.
March 1892

Index

A

Abbate
  Angelia Phyllis 134
Abruzzo
  Anthony 116
  Eric Cameron 116
  John 116
  John Mark 116
Acorn
  Fred 79
Adams
  Debra 87
  Gail 62
  Janice 108
Adzick
  Sharon 82
Affleck
  Margaret 41
  Rose 73
Agnew
  Gary 84
  Kyle 84
  Leta Dona 84
Allen
  Cullen Rae 78
  Priscilla 134
Anderson
  Erin 38
  Evelyne 41
  Garfield 38
  Glen 38
  Kurt 38
Andreason
  Amber 67
  Bjorn 66
  Starla 67
Ansonen
  Anna Sophia 45
Archibald
  Clara 82
Armand
  Anne 135
Armstrong
  Jeff 108
Arthur
  Colin George 71
  David Bertram 72
  Kimberley Anne 72
  Stephen 72
Austin
  Eleanor 141
Avison
  Molly Nora Louise 163

B

Babb
  Alan 84
  Jamie Leroy 84
  Ken 84
Babineau
  Ronald 64
Bagnall
  Elizabeth 118
  Mezena 118
Bailey
  Kimberly 134
  Meredith 134
  Ray 134
Bain
  Brandon 96
  Jessica 96
  Kaleb 96
  Timothy 96
Baker
  Katie 133
  Leith 133
  Weston Allen 133
Ballem
  Carolyn Jane 69
  Cedric 67
  Christopher Gordon 69
  Evelyn Elizabeth 67
  James Wayne 68
  Jarrod Wayne 68
  John Charles 68
  Joshua William 68
  Linda Pauline 68
  Marsha Lynne 68
  Michael Ivan 69
  Myrna Belle 67
Bane
  Donald 15
Banfill
  Douglas 92
  Roger 92
  Walter 92
  Wendy 92
Banks
  Clement 89
  Donald 75, 88
  Doris 75
  Elva 75
  Janice 76, 89
  Jean 89
  John 60, 76, 88, 89
  Lloyd 70
  Margaret 75
  Minnie Alberta 89
  Paul 75
  Rebecca 59
  Russell 89
  Warren 89
  Wilbur 75, 76
  Willard 88
Banner
  Betty 156
Barker
  Robin 93

Barrett
　Judith 43
Barry
　Jackie 64
Bartelt
　Margarete 94
Bastin
　C.E. 41
　F.M. 40
　May 41
Bateman
　Robert 150
Bates
　Candice Jean 121
Bauer
　Shanea 116
Beale
　Linda 35
Bears
　Alfreda 118
　Eleanor 37
　George 51
　John 118
Beaton
　Linda 63
Beck
　Jennie 92
Belanger
　Brooke Aimee 120
　Guy Robert 120
　Joshua Guy 120
　Sara Eva 120
Bell
　Nicholas Bar-
　　tholomew 86
　Scott Alexander 86
　Stuart MacIntosh 86
　Warren 86
　William Wryley 86
Belsen
　Lily 120

Bengert
　Teddi Kim 117
Bennett
　Bert 142
　Betty Lou 142
　David 132
　James 142
　JoAnne Rachel 142
　John 142
　Kendra 132
　Laura 94
　Richard 132, 142
　Sally 142
　Sterndale 153
　William Richard
　　142
Bierens
　Linda 137
Bigelow
　Heather 91
Black
　Jenna 66
　Matthew 66
　Ronald 66
Blackett
　Robert Aaron 115
　Robert Bruce 115
　Valen Rose 115
Blatch
　Allan 44
　John 44
　Philip 44
　Ted 44
Bogstie
　Wendy 127
Bohnert
　Cynthia 87
Bond
　Barbara May 86
　Jeanine Catherine
　　86
　Ken 86

Milda 77
Bonin
　Heather Jean 88
Bonner
　Paul Stephen 67
Boswell
　Brenda 65
　Christine Lothian
　　65
　Christopher John
　　65
　Irving 65
　Irving Lorne 65
　Matthew David 65
　Nicholas Jay 65
　Sheila Blanche 65
Boswick
　Joan 75
Bouchard
　Tami Jane 82
Bowen
　Catherine 40
　Norman L. 40
Bowles
　Anne 93
Bowley
　Anna 38
　Colin 38
　Deanna 37
　Eric 38
　George 37
　Gregory 38
　James 38
　Joan 38
　Nicolle 38
　Preston 37
　Richard 38
　Ryan 38
　Stephen 38
　Wayne 37
Bradford
　Teresa 135

Bradley
  Noreen 70
Brightman
  Dean 79
  Diana 79
  Thomas 79
Brothers
  Augustine 62
Brown
  Julie 155
  Mary Elizabeth 139
  Shelly 32
  Teresa Joan 72
  Virginia 128
Bruce
  Ann 53
  Malcolm 53
  Murdoch 53
  Murdock 54
Bruvold
  Boyd Melvin 80
  Kelsey 80
  Nicole Katherine 80
Burch
  Don 70
Burke
  Karen 72
Burns
  Debbie 37
  James 37
  Richelle 63
  Robert 63
Burris
  Tex 78
Bussey
  Dot 129
Buzzell
  James 133
Byck
  Alexandra 62
  David 62
  Shawn 62

C

Cameron
  Alex. 174
  Ann 106
  Arnold 106
  Douglas 95
  John 174
  Katelyn 106
  Linda 95
  Martin Richard 95
  Samuel 106
  Wayne 95
Campbell
  Abraham Samuel 127
  Amy Pearl 127
  Andrea Rebecca 127
  Ashley Elizabeth 127
  Caroline Olive 163
  Catherine Isabella 163
  Cathy 128
  Clarence 129
  Corey Jean 128
  David James 127
  Della 39
  Derek Roy 128
  Donald 136
  Donald Kenneth 127
  Donald Roy 127
  Douglas James 127
  Duncan 164
  Edith 125, 136
  Eva 129
  Evelyn 129
  Florence 128
  Garnett Weldon 162
  Genevieve Ma-

rie-France 128
  Heather 128
  Hugh Archibald 163
  Ian 128
  James Andrew 162
  James 127, 128
  James Murdoch 163
  Jemima 163
  John 125, 126, 127, 129
  John Robert Lamont 163
  John William 127
  Julien-Anne Grace 128
  Katie 163
  Maria Elise 127
  Marilyn Jane 127
  Michael Dale 127
  Rebecca 127, 128
  Robert 163
  Roy 113, 127, 128
  Samuel Ewen 127
  Samuel John 127
  Sheldon 129
  Simon Thomas 127
  Vernon J. 162
  William Isaac 127
Campion
  Ava 113
  Ava Joan 115
  David Alexander 116
  David Mark 116
  Dennis Andrew 115
  Dennis Ernest 115
  Hannah Lynn 116
  Julie Margaret 115
  Murray Taylor 116
  Rachel Mae 116

Sarah Anne 116
Canavan
  Brendan 107
Canmore
  Gladys 77
Cantelo
  Catherine 39
  John 39
Cardin
  Johanne 154
Carisle
  Winnifred 135
Chabot
  Terrahynn 84
  Wes 83
Chartier
  Shannon Marie 121
Chessor
  David 32
  Ian 32
Chetek
  Sandra 33
Christie
  Ann 13
Cirone
  Antonio 35
  Joseph Frederico 35
Clark
  Arnold Thomas 122
  Ashley Lyn 122
  Daryl Thomas 122
  Jared 157
  Jeff 156
  Kimberly Ann 122
  Thomas 122, 157
Clarke
  Austin Clarke 151
Cleland
  Alan 155
  Briony 155
  Eilidh 155
  James 155

JoAnne 155
Kate 155
Kirsty 155
Martin 155
Millar 155
Murray 155
Rachael 155
Robert 155
Cloyd
  David 133
  Ruth 133
  Starr Ann 133
Coates
  Coady 39
  Rebecca 39
  Terry 39
Cohen
  Nathan 153
Coleman
  Ruth 127
Colling
  John 45
Compton
  Albert Wayne 70
  Catherine 99
  Catherine Violet 70
  Charles Reginald 70
  Christopher John 97
  Daniel James 97
  David 95, 96, 98
  Doris Elaine 70
  Ellie 140
  Esther 96
  Ewen MacDougall 96
  Heather 99
  James 97
  James Wellington 96, 97
  John 51, 97
  Judy 97

Kayleigh 99
Kevin 99
Leeland Grant 70
Lemuel 144
Lisa 99
Lucy Anne 144
Malcolm Henry 96
Margaret Etta 70
Margaret Jane 144
Mary Matilda (Tilly) 98, 123
Paul 99
Philip 97
Philip Kevin 99
Reginald 70
Rhona 99
Ronald 97
Steven 99
Tilly 98, 123
Travis James 97
Tyler Franklin 97
Wendy 97
Cook
  Joseph 174
Cooper
  Lillan Grace Rona 104
Corsano
  Elissa 103
Corzine
  Christopher Scott 142
  Jack W. 142
  Jeffrey Allan 142
  Julie Beth 143
Coyle
  Helen 35
Crawley
  Budge 153
Creed
  Caleb 119
  Reuben 119

Cross
  Alexandre Frederick 76
  Arthur Frederick 76
  Bonnie 76
  Christina Marie 77
  Douglas 76
  Douglas Marcel 76
  Earl 77
  Karen Kimberly 76
  Michael 77
  Rachel Ileana 77
  Susan 76
  Sylvia Frances 77
Crozier
  Robert 67
Cudmore
  Donald 105
  Eddie 105
  Karen 105
  Kevin 105
Cummings
  Dan 35
  David 35
  Donald 35
  Tracy 35
Currie
  Adina Lynn 88
  Aileen 155
  Marlow 88
  Mary 27, 57
  Nolan Marlow 88
  Sarah 110
Cutcliffe
  Hilda 162
Cymbaluk
  Abrienne Kierra 81
  Amy Jo-Anne 81
  Brisa Jane 81
  Caetria Karis 81
  Gary Martin 81
  Gregg Loyd 80

  Jeffrey Theodore 81
  Jordon Kevin 81
  Kamilla 81
  Kevin Patrick 80
  Kristen Jo-Anne 81
  Leon Martin 81
  Thadden Elis 81
  Theodore 80, 81

D

Darrach
  Aubrey 119
  Canaan 119
  Christopher 119
  Hunter 119
  Melanie 113, 119
David
  Golda 92
  Jaban 92
  James 92
  Kea 92
  Natasha 92
  Tekoa 92
Davis
  Cynthia Ann 34
Dawe
  Doris 90
Dawes
  Alexandra 64
  Peter 64
  Troy 64
Deeran
  Alexandrea Elizabeth 117
  Randy Deeran 116
DeGanahl
  Brice 157
  Carl Brice 157
  Donald Andrew 157
  Sheila 157

  Wendy 157
Delladance
  Rene 36
Denton
  Leslie 85
Derring
  Ben 72
DesRoche
  Pauline 117
Deyell
  W.J. 47
Dimond
  Fred 162
Dobeck
  Louise 141
Docherty
  Alexander 36
  Cyril 36
  Denise 36
  Elaine 36
  Erin 36
  Florence 34
  Glen 35
  Jeffery 35
  Jonathon 36
  Kenneth 36
  Louise 35
  Margaret 35
  Matthew 37
  Shane 36
  Sonia 36
  Wellington N. 34
  Willard 35
Dodson
  Alan 102
  Anne Elizabeth 102
  Aubrey 102
  Bruce 102
  Catherine Elizabeth 102
  David 103
  Doreen 103

Kevin 102
Orlar Aubrey 102
Sharon 102
Wilbur 102
William 102, 103
Donaldson
  Keith 102
  Sarah 102
Doucett
  Susan 76
Douglas
  J. Lester 122
Drake
  Alexander 62
  Pearl 62
  Wendell 47
  William 62
Driscoll
  Jason 128
  Joseph 128
  Vanessa 128
Duff
  Donald 174
Duncan
  Gregory 106
  Hannah 106
Dupont
  Fred 144

E

Easter
  Beryl Gertrude 62
Edwards
  Carl Robert 73
  David Earl 72
  Donna Vera 72
  Jackie Walter 72
  Joan Elaine 73
  Judy Ann 72
  Norma Jean 72
  Walter John 72

Ellingson
  Kim Lori 121
Elsass
  Sarah Beth 81
Elwood
  Michael 72
Erickson
  Josh 86
Ervick
  Anne 79
Ervine
  Eileen 133
Essam
  Richard James Llewellyn 106
  Stephen 106
Estifjord
  Ivor 35
  Jane 35
Evans
  Shirley Ann 142
Ewart
  Alan 83
  Charles 84
  Daniel 83
  Danielle Dawn 83
  Jean 84
  Judy 84
  Kimberly Laine 83
  Leta 84
  Neil 84

F

Fallow
  Adrian 32
  Alexander 32
  Lynn 32
  Rod 32
  Tracy 32
  Vanessa 32
  William 32

Fanning
  Lois 34
Ferguson
  Barbara Jean 70
  Brenda 70
Fiest
  Linda 82
  Lyndon 82
  Michael 82
Fleming
  David 128
  Elizabeth 128
  Jack 128
  Rebecca Fleming 128
Floyd
  Joshua Kyle 86
  Kyle William 86
Fookes
  Arnold William 74
  Catherine Faye 74
  Lyle William 74
  Robert Bradley 74
  Ronald Alexander 74
Foster
  Lauren 94
Fraser
  William 174
Freeze
  Catherine 94
  David 94
  Emily Elizabeth 64
  George 94
  Hannah Catherine 94
  Jacob George 94
  Jillian 64
  John David 94
  Ralph 64
  Rebecca 64
  Samuel MacLeod 94

Friesen
  Jessie Dale 84
  Roy 84
  Tiffany Alexandria 84
Frizzell
  Aaron James 72
  Cecil Leslie 73
  Connor 72
  Dana Lillian 71
  David Vernon 71
  Diane Christena 73
  Donald Ivan 71
  George Edison 71
  Helen Anne 72
  Ivan Lemuel 71
  James Donald 71
  James Robert Andrew 72
  Jasmine Grace 71
  Jenna Faith 71
  Jennifer Liane 71
  Kelly Anne 71
  Leslie Sterling 73
  Lorelei Glenda 71
  Lorna Mae 71
  Mark Dean 72
  Matthew James 72
  Nicholas 72
  Paul William 71
  Randy George 71
  Rita 70
  Roger Dean 72
  Ronald Edward 71
  Samuel 72
  Stephen 71
  Vanessa 71
  Vernon Wilfred 71
  Warren James 72
  Winnifred Angela 72

Froese
  Douglas John 121
  Matthew MacLeod 121
  Mya Nicole 121
Furness
  David 93
  Donald 93
  Jason 93
  Kathy 93
  Lauren 93
  Lee David 93
  Russell 93
  Sheila 93
Futer
  Pamela 41

G

Gabal
  Ray 87
Gale
  Bonnie Lee 122
Garnhum
  Joni 119
Gaudet
  Paulette 70
Gauthier
  Judith Helene 67
Geddes
  Betty 99
  Dianne 89
  Eldon 89
  Garry 89
  James 89
Ghazarossian
  Alex 96
Gibbs
  James Alfred 75
  Reginald 75
Gibson
  Douglas 151

Gildert
  Joelle 68
Gillespie
  Viola 91
Gillingham
  Kenneth 79
  Laura 79
  Robert 79
  Walter 79
Gillis
  Alec 111
  Alexander 104, 105
  Ann Louise 106
  Archie 106
  Carol 107
  Catherine Anne 104
  David Gordon 108
  David Roy 108
  Donald 104, 105
  Donna 105
  Dorothy 106
  Dwayne 105
  Elizabeth Ann 108
  Elizabeth 109
  Elizabeth Joyce 106
  Ewen Lamont 108
  George Warren 104
  Glenda 106
  Gordon 106, 108
  Gordon James 106
  Grant 105
  Jessie 89
  Joan Marion 107
  John Alexander 104
  John D. Gillis 111
  John 106, 109, 111
  Katie 104
  Margaret 105, 108, 109
  Mary 105, 111
  Mary K. 111

INDEX

Mary Rachel 105
Pamela Margaret 108
Roger 113
Ross 105
Sadie 105, 111
Sarah 105
William 53, 89, 107
Glandon
  Judy Acorn 79
Glover
  Cindy Lou 66
  Danielle Anne 67
  Deborah Anne 66
  Jason 66
  Kara 67
  Kyle 67
  Michael 67
  Stephen Paul 67
  Travis Stephen 67
Goguen
  Pauline Gloria 71
Gohm
  David 105
Golden
  Grant 141
  James 141
Goodman
  Brian 142
Goodwill
  John 50, 53, 170, 201, 202, 203, 205
  Tom 170
Gordon
  Jubal Jeramiah 86
  Katherine Joy 86
  William 86
Graham
  Chelsea Michelle 121
  Dena Lynn 121

Don 70
Glenda 38
Kaleb Matthew 121
Keith David 121
Robert David 121
Tiffany Leanne 121
Tyler David 121
Grant
  George 116
Green
  Joan 63
Griffin
  Chad 38
Guretzki
  Carla 84
  Corrine Melany 84
  Joseph 84, 85
  Landon Joseph 85
  Tamara Charlene 84

H

Hagen
  Edith Violet 45
  Lillian Virginia 45
Hamilton
  A.L. 47
  Arthur Lee 46
Hampson
  Lynne 85
Haramic
  Joseph Jon 77
  Joseph Michael 77
  Nicole Renee 77
Harms
  Geoffrey Joseph 77
Harper
  Adam 118
  Harley 118
  Jonathan 118
Harrington

Betty 140
Harris
  Maida 127
Harty
  Aaron 135
  Don 135
  Jeri 135
Haskell
  Alice 77
Hatfield
  Shirley 132
Hayes
  Margaret 127
Hayter
  Eileen 105
  Sandra 87
Head
  Maude 102
Henwood
  Sandra 66
Heritage
  Frances 157
Hernstead
  Lillian 87
  Renee 87
Heseleton
  Robert 75
Hicken
  Teena 36
Hill
  Andrew Taylor 69
  David 69
  Robert 69
Hilton
  Lulu 154. See also Louise Jack
Hince
  Eveline Marie 76
Hogg
  Charlotte Anne 66
  David Ralph 66

Timothy David 66
Holly
  Louise 102
Honeybourne
  Amanda 154
  Derek 154
  Patricia 154
Horne
  Sylvia 83
Horvath
  Monique Candace 107
  Stephen John 107
Howe
  Heidi 134
Hrycak
  Andrew 81
  Anita Lynn 81
  Ashlee Dawn 81
  Ivan 81
  Joshua 81
  Karen Denice 81
  Sarah Jean 81
Hudson
  Alison Mary Lynn 83
  David Eugene Hubert 83
  David 83
  Devin Lamont 83
  Eileen Jessie 83
  Eliza Amelia 83
  Ellen Frances Eloise Catherine 83
  Elsa Suzannah 83
  Emily Sarah 83
  Erin Maria 83
  Esther Isabella 83
  Melissa Kathleen 83
  Samuel George 83
  Sharlene Rosalie 83
Hume
  Aaron 138
  Allen 134
  Allison 135
  Brandon 135
  Bruce 139
  Carol 134
  Catherine 131
  Catherine Lamont 138
  Cathy 137
  Colin 139
  David 139, 143
  Debby 134
  Derek 139
  Donald 134, 137, 138, 139
  Donna 135
  Effie Anne 149
  Elizabeth 138, 139, 142
  Elmer 134
  Emily 140
  Ethan 137
  Euphemia Ann 25, 145
  Ewen Hume 133, 144
  Florence Nightingale 144
  George 139
  Gladys Dorothy 134
  Isabella 134, 137
  James 135
  Jeffery 139
  Jessica 135
  Jillian 136
  Johanna 139
  John A. 131
  John Alexander 133
  John Hume 80, 130, 134, 137, 145, 148
  John S. 145
  John Willie 137, 138
  Joseph 139, 143, 148
  Joshua 138
  JT 135
  Judy 139
  Karen Elizabeth 139
  Kathleen 139
  Kieren 137
  Laura 136
  Linda Diane 139
  Linda 135
  Lloyd 134
  Margaret Frances 144
  Margaret 136, 142
  Marla Anne 139
  Mary Alice 133
  Matthew 139
  Michael 135, 138
  Nicholas 135
  Penelope Taylor 133
  Richard 135
  Richard Scott 135
  Robert 135
  Sam 130, 148
  Samuel 136
  Sandra 134
  Sarah Frances 140
  Sarah 80, 83, 135
  Sarah Margaret 136
  Sean 139
  Stacy 139
  Stuart 139
  Tommy 134
  Wendy 135

INDEX

William Ewen 133
Hungle
  Ronald 108
Hurdle
  Sheila 105
Hurry
  Anne Lorraine 62
  Audrey Elizabeth 63
  Carolyn Gertrude 62
  Charles 62, 63
  David Charles 63
  Davin 63
  Frances Carolyn 64
  Jessie 62
  Lacey 62
  Lorna Jeanine 63
  Miriam Roberta 64
  Paul Sidney 62
  Sidney Charles 62
Hussey
  Irene 35
Hutchison
  Jarin 82
  Joel 82
  Rick 82

I

Irons
  Samantha 99
Irving
  Amanda 67
  Brent 67
  Brodie Sanderson 67

J

Jack
  Donald 150, 151
  Louise 150
  Lulu 150
  Maren 150, 154
  Marjorie 154
  Mary 150
  Nancy 153
  Nicholas Martin Lamont 154
  Robert M. 154
  R.P. 150
Jackson
  Cathy 37
Jamieson
  Lorelle 122
Jardine
  Diane Hazel 71
Jasper
  Angela Dawn 120
  Kenneth Reuben 120
  MacKenzie Cheyenne 120
  Michael Scott 120
  Rueben Ernest 120
  Shelly Joan Leeanne 120
Jenkins
  Emily 109
Jensen
  Erna 82
  Ivhis 77
John of the Lilacs. See John Robert Lamont Campbell
Johnson
  James 62
  Olivia 62
Johnstone
  Barbara Anne 66
Jones
  Kurt 81

K

Karjouski
  Sheri Lynn 35
Karp
  Hilda 88
Kassar
  Gabriel 41
Keefe
  Austin 116
  Michael 116
  Spencer Campbell 116
Keenan
  Elizabeth 117
Keilani
  Nabil 157
  Nadia 157
  Reema 157
Kemshead
  Davin Edward Lawrence 85
  Larry 85
  Megan Jan 85
Keown
  Ronda 141
Kidston
  Catherine 140
  Emma Jean 140
  Jessie 140
  Teddy Louis 140
  William Arthur 140
  William 140
Kinck
  Phyllis 138
King
  Barbara 78
  Bill 78
  Bob 78
  Brian 77
  Carol Ann 78
  Celia Frances 76

Celia Lynn 77
Diane 78
Donna 78
F. 60
Frederick Elias 76, 77
Fred 77
Janice 78
John Ewen 78
Lois 78
Marguerite Elizabeth 78
Marilyn Louise 78
Mary Elizabeth 78
Michael 78
Patrick 77
Richard Alexander 77
Richard Earl 78
Sandy 135
Sharon 77
Kirkland
  Michael 43
Kitson
  Glenda Erna 71
Knaull
  Jessica 72
  Krista 72
  Robert 72
Knowsley
  Wendy 117
Kourakos
  George 106
  Jonathon Matthew Malcolm 107
  Julie Ann 107
Krawchuk
  Catherine Elizabeth 102
  Cathy 102
  David 102

Kreplin
  Martin Jost 69
  Matthew West 69
  Sarah Lynn 69
Kuelne
  Rachel Allison 80
Kuhn
  Brian Richard 120
  Jesse Michael 120
  Justin Richard 120
  Tyler Matthew 120
Kurylo
  Matthew 85
  Nicole 85

L

Ladan
  Aubrey David 88
  Cassidy Marie 88
  Terry Aubrey 88
Ladner
  Catherine 33
Lamb
  Barbara 98, 123
Lamond. See Lamont
Lamont
  Alexandra 43
  Allen 150
  Andrew 41
  Angus Charles 45
  Angus 29, 31, 46, 47, 54, 100, 101, 102, 103
  Ann 103, 150, 153
  Benjamin 39
  Bruce 162
  Caris 157
  Carrie 46
  Cassie 163
  Catherine Jane 163
  Catherine Jean 41
  Catherine 10, 43, 46, 93, 103, 130, 138, 139, 162
  Catherine Margaret 163
  Catriona Margaret 157
  Charles Edward 42
  Charles 42, 45
  Chester Ronald 44
  Christina 162
  Christopher John 103
  Christy Mary 32
  Daniel 34
  David Henry 157
  David 148. 155
  Debra 39
  D.M. 147, 159, 160, 171
  Donald Ian 156
  Donald 26, 29, 34, 37, 39, 53, 56, 148, 153, 156, 158, 159, 162, 167
  Donald M. 148
  Donald MacDonald 158, 159
  Donna 39
  Dougald 43
  Douglas 39
  Edward 42, 43
  Effie Ann 148
  Eleanor 38
  Elizabeth 31, 43, 46, 80, 95, 103, 129, 130, 156
  Elspeth 155
  Elvira Elsie 44
  Ena 158

Index

Euphemia 44
Ewen Alexander 162
Ewen 1, 8, 34, 47, 48, 49, 51, 54, 56, 57, 58, 59, 61, 83, 89, 93, 98, 100, 101, 103, 104, 108, 139, 140, 144, 145, 148. 155, 161, 162, 164, 172, 205
Frances 43, 54, 58, 59, 61, 136, 150
Frances Margaret 103
Francis Bastin 43
Gillane 37
Iris 162
Isabella 37, 163
Jacob 39
James 23, 32, 161
Jason Ewen 103
Jean 34, 41
John Ernest MacLeod 103
John Gordon 46
John 32, 43, 44, 46, 47, 95, 100, 103
John Ryan 104
John Salmon 40, 41
Jonathon Craig 103
Jonathon 39
Katherine Belle 155
Katie 148
Laura 43
Lillian 149
Lizzie 32, 46, 47
Madeleine 41

Malcolm 14, 28, 29, 31, 37, 39, 44, 45, 47, 89, 90, 133, 148, 156, 161, 162
Margaret Anne 161
Margaret 44, 103, 157, 161, 162, 163
Maria 41
Marjory 34
Mary Catherine 93
Mary Elizabeth 80, 103, 130
Mary Jane 163
Mary Jannet 34
Mary 32, 40, 41, 42, 129, 130, 131
Matthew 39
M.B. 46
Murdina 158
Murdoch 26, 29, 56, 145, 147, 149, 161, 162
Murdoch William 163
Murdock 28, 32, 53, 54
Peggy 37
Peter 162
Preston 44
Rebecca 7, 58, 110, 125
Rhona 155
Robert 150, 163
Ronald 31, 34, 44
Ruth 37
Sadie 46
Sam 148
Samuel 149, 150
Sarah Ann 150, 153
Sarah Isabella 37

Sarah 34, 44, 45, 46, 47, 90, 102, 104, 160
Silas 31
Thelma 155
Veda 44
Virginia 156
W.D. 55
William Dawson 13, 24, 25, 156
William D. 145
William 29, 30, 32, 93, 148, 163
Lanegraff
  Ellen 150
Larkin
  Gail 93
LaRue
  Chantal 96
Leafe
  Francesca 122
  Ian S. 122
  Marion 112
  Mary 113, 123
LeDrew
  Alfred 102
  Gina Lynn 102
  Laura Louise 102
Lee
  Brian 82
  Corrina Nora 82
  Deanna Marie 82
  Karen 129
Lennox
  George 41
  Mariah 41
Leskin
  Tim 81
Letts
  Alexis 64
  Nelson 64

Lewis
  Colby Chadburn 64
  Jodi Mae 64
  Katelyn Brittney 64
  Margaret Elizabeth 65
  Marilyn 119
  Melanie Jean 64
  Morgan Harrison 64
  Ross Albert 64
  Sydney Carolyn 64
  Thomas Charles 64
Lind
  Joyce 87
  Leslie 87
  Lois 87
  Marjory 87
Ling
  Judy Beth 81
Linneberg
  Cody Maurice Alexander 105
  Karen 162
  Maurice 105
Lofthouse
  Eunice 154
Long
  Christina Louise 69
  Gordon William 69
  Jane 44
  Jennie 44
  Maureen Elizabeth 69
  Sharon Mary-Lee 69
Lord
  Jessie 91
Lothian
  Christine 65
Love
  Donna Maureen 64
  Gordon Francis 64
  Lorelei Margaret 64
  Noreen Roberta 64
Lowry
  Cliff 84
  Delaina Lynn 85
  Dennis Raymond 85
  Iris Isabel 85
  Mavis June 84
  Patrick Skye 85
  Shon 85
Ludwick
  Betty Jean 131
  Dallas Esdrus 131
Lundell
  Robert 135
Lyons
  Charles 75
  Doris Margaret 75
  James Alfred 75

M

Mabin
  Eleanor 141
MacAree
  Terry 39
MacBeth
  Jessie 118
MacCallien Mor 13
MacCallum
  Pauline 67
MacColl
  James 50
MacDonald
  Adam 34
  Alexander 33, 67, 68
  Amanda Jean 38
  Andrew 38
  Andrew William
  Cedric 68
  Angusina 156
  Angus 27, 28
  Brian Douglas 67
  Carolyn 67
  Carter 34
  Catherine Helene 67
  Chelsea 33
  Christina 31
  Craig 38
  Daniel 33
  Dannie 119
  Donald Elmer 33
  Donald John 105
  Donald 28, 33, 38, 48, 50, 51, 53, 54, 56, 101, 145, 158, 159, 164, 166, 169, 184
  Donald Richard 33
  Dorothy 69
  Douglas Blair 67
  Dustin 34
  Elizabeth 28, 29, 31, 38, 44, 47, 65, 67
  Frances 28
  Garry 39
  Gladys 38
  Hughie James 65
  Jackson Franklin 65
  Jamin Glen Irving 65
  Jean 38, 135
  Jenna Elizabeth 65
  Jennifer Grace 68
  Jennifer 34
  Joanne 34
  Jodi 113

Index

Jody 119
John Findlay 105
John Ronald 32
Joseph 33
Justin Hughie 65
Kari Lynn 38
Katie Ann 33
Keith Blair 33
Keith Michael 34
Kelli Joan 68
Kenneth 38
Kimberly 116, 119
Lachlan 31
Lloyd 113
Mallory 34
Mark 116
Mary 31, 32
Michelle Lee 116
Moody 38
Myron Franklin 65
Neil 39, 119
Norman 7, 137
Peter 105
Rachel 113
Rebecca JoAnne 68
Robert James 67
Robert 39
Roderick 32, 33
Ronald 32, 33
Sally 105
Sandy 67
Sarah Elizabeth 65
Stacy Ellen 116
Stephen Bernard 68
Stephen Troy 68
Sterling Leigh 33
Steven 36, 38
Stuart 33
Susan 71
Taxi Dan 32, 33
Taylor 39
Timothy John 68
Troy 68, 70
Wendy Elizabeth 67
William Duff 39
William 33
MacDougall
  Amy Christine 35
  Ashley Joan 35
  Carrie Ann 34
  Corey Steven 35
  Courtney Nicole 34
  David 34
  Diane 37
  Edmond 142
  Ewen 96, 124
  Gordon 34
  Janet 35
  Jeffrey Scott 143
  Lester B. 142
  Linda Joyce 142
  Linda 35
  Margaret 102
  Nancy 35
  Philip Whitfield 35
  Phillip 35
  Scott Gregory 143
  Tyler Roberts 143
MacEachern
  John 51, 52
  Lindsay 63
  Margaret 34, 37
  Mark 63
  Stephanie 63
  Terry 63
MacEwen
  Margaret J. 163
  Walford 163
MacFadzen
  Jessie Anne 66
  Mark 66
  Tyler Mark 66
MacGillivary
  Isabel 116
MacGowan
  James 155
Macintosh
  Margaret 88
MacIntosh
  Agnes 103
  Alexander 59, 61, 74, 79, 82, 136
  Amanda Jean 88
  Autumn Paris Jensen 82
  Belinda Lee 80
  Bonnie Lynn 80
  Bradley Victor 82
  Chance Travis 82
  Charlotte Fay 88
  Christina Marie 83
  Christine Frances 61
  Christine 69
  Cody William 82
  Colin 87
  Dale Lamont 81
  Daniel 103
  Darrell Charles 83
  David 88
  Donald 60, 80, 83, 86, 131, 136
  Donald William 80
  Donna 83, 88
  Douglas Murray 82
  Edith Alberta 83
  Effie 103
  Emerson 87
  Eva Frances 80
  Ewen Lamont 83
  Ewen 74
  Frances 61, 80, 88
  Gary Donald 86
  Gladys Isabel 84
  Glen Stuart 82
  Hazel Isabelle 79

Holly Dale 81
Ian Douglas 80
J.A. 60
Janis Kim 86
Jo-Anne Alberta 80
John Angus 76
John Ludovick 80
Judy Lynn 85
Karen Donna 88
Katherine Mavis 86
Kathleen Joan 83
Kayla Ruby 88
Laurie Lamont 79
Lawrence 85
Lillian 87, 136
Margaret 61
Margaret Ann 75
Marilyn Carol 83
Mark Donald 86
Marlene Loralie 81
Mary Elizabeth 82
Merrily Joan 81
Murdock 87
Murray Dwayne 82
Raymond Alan 88
Rebecca 76, 88
Renae 87
Renaldo Vachel 81
Reta Margaret 86
Richard Lee 78
Richard 59, 81
Rita 74
Robert 59, 60
Rodney William 82
Sandra Jean 82
Sarah 76
Sean Garry 86
Sherilyn Elizabeth 80
Shirley Patricia 80
Tammy 82
Wayne David 88

William Alexander 79, 82
Macintyre
  Duncan 173
MacIntyre
  Claude 37
  Edith 37
  Elwood 38
  Mary 133
  Michele 38
  Reta 37
  Rollie 37
  Sydney 37
MacIsaac
  Alexander 106
  Greg 105
  Lorna 97
MacKay
  Bobby 33
  Gloria 33
  Jessie Catherine 163
MacKenzie
  Eliza B. 147
  Flora 99
  James 161
  Jean 91
  J. 147
  M. 55
MacKinnon
  Alex 91
  Carl 118
  Catherine 31
  Christina 162
  Cyrus 31
  Daniel 31
  Duncan 31
  Ewen 31
  Flora 31
  Hazel 118
  Lachlan 31
  Malcolm 31

Mary 31, 39
Ronald 31
Sarah 31
MacLean
  Cynthia E. 68
  Darryl 39
  Elizabeth 116
  Marshall 39
  Morgan 39
MacLellan
  Ann 118
  Jean 118
MacLeod
  Alexander Wesley 93
  Amanda 119
  Amelia Danielle 122
  Andrea May 121
  Andrew Hector 122
  Angus A.A.J. 93
  Anne 95, 118, 119, 121
  Ann 108
  Arianne Elizabeth 122
  Brittany Laurel 122
  Carley Anne 121
  Catherine 31
  Charles 50, 113, 114, 122
  Charles Reginald 118
  Christa 119
  Christy 31, 89
  Cody Stephen Francis 98, 123
  Connor Malcolm 94
  Curtis Roderick 122
  Daniel Peter 122

Index

Darrell 119
Darren 119
David Cartwright 122
David 93, 94
Dean Thomas 122
Donald John 104
Donald 31, 119
Dorothy 93
Elinor 95
Ella 70, 112, 114, 115, 123, 124
Ellen Elizabeth 115
Ernest 103, 113, 118
Euphemia 44
Ewen Angus 123
Ewen 112, 113, 119
Flora 37, 136
Florence 118
Gladys 94
Glen William 94
Harold 112
Harold Blair 94
Harold S. 1, 2, 6, 98, 123
Hector 112, 119, 122
Ian 118
Ina 95
Isabel 93
Jalen Taylor 95
James 94
Janet Rebecca 118
Janis Lynn 123
Janis 98
Janna Lee 121
Jenna Elyssa MacLeod 94
Jennifer Joy 122
Jessica 119
Joan Margaret 34

Joan Miriam 120
John Henry 54
John 35, 104
John Michael 94
John Walter 94, 111
Jolynn Ashlee 121
Jonathan Paul 121
Judith Margaret 120
Kaley Melissa 95
Kayla Marie 121
Keillier 94
Kenneth Martin 95
Kieran Alexander 94
Leland James Foster 94
Leon 94
Linda 93
Linda Margaret 121
Lisa Beverly 122
Luke Anthony 122
Malcolm Kenneth 95
Margaret 111
Margaret Anne 118
Marion Rachel 122
Mark 94
Mary 95, 119
Matthew Barnet 121
Michael 51, 94
Michelle 95
Murdina 137
Pamela Anne 95
Paul Roderick 121
Peter 94, 122
Rachelle Nicole 122
Rebecca Lynn 122
Reg 112
Rhoda Maxine 94
Robert Andrew 94
Roderick Alexander 113
Roderick Charles (Roddie Charlie) 113, 114, 122
Roderick C. 112, 113
Roderick MacKinnon 118
Roderick 113, 121, 122
Ryan 119
Samuel Jamieson 122
Shannon 119
Stephen Ross 98, 123
Tilly 123
Timothy Roger 122
Wendell 112
Wendell Murdock 118
Wendy Lynn 121
Whitefield 34
MacMillan
  Allan 142
  Gloria 72
  Phyllis Mary Jane 69
  Ryan 79
MacMurdo
  Edward B. 163
MacMurray
  E.J. 40
MacNeill
  Archie Silas 110
  Edith 125, 127
  Ella 123, 124
  Hugh 123
  Margaret 7, 111
  Mary 123
  Murdoch 125

Murdock 110
Sarah 111
MacNevin
  Charles 144
  Christine 145
  Joseph 145
MacPhail
  Adam 63
  Angela 63
  Brandon Alan 63
  Carol Elizabeth 63
  Ellen 63
  Erin 63
  John Wayne 63
  Kenneth Charles 63
  Leslie Alan 63
  Leslie Willard 63
  Mathew 63
  Sarah 63
  Shelly Rotha 63
  Sir Andrew 49, 61, 89
  Virginia Louise 63
  William 48, 49
MacPhee
  Malcolm 37
  Margaret 37
  Wanda Isabel 70
MacPherson
  Alice 132
  Archibald 91
  Arthur 91
  Catherine Elizabeth 100
  Catherine 102
  Charles 91
  Christina 76
  Christine 91
  Darren MacPherson 92
  Donald 90
  Dorothy 132
  Duncan 91
  Edith 36
  Elizabeth 100, 131
  Evelyn 92
  Geraldine 92
  Harold 132
  Ian 91
  Isabella 133
  James 132
  Jessie 91
  John 27, 57, 92
  Kay 106
  Kimble 92
  Lamont 91
  Laura 92
  Leah 92
  Lila 92
  Lynn 78
  Malcolm "George" 106
  Mark 91
  Martin 92
  Mary 132
  Michael 150
  Pamela 132
  Richard 131
  Robert 92
  Sandy 132
  Sarah 25, 56, 57, 58, 59, 89, 100, 104, 139, 161
  Shirley 92
  Thelma Ann 150
MacQueen
  Malcolm 26, 28, 29, 48, 56
Madson
  Joan 67
Makaroff
  Christine 43
  Douglas 43
  Jonathan 43
  Michael 43
Manner
  Charles 106
Marchessault
  Marie-Claude 128
Marshall
  Allyson 65
  Ashley 65
  Jason 65
  Leonard 65
  Norma 103
Martell
  George David Draper 103
  Lamont 103
  Margaret 103
  Muriel Elizabeth 103
  Phyllis Marie 103
  Roy Ewen 103
Martin
  Emily. See Jenkins: Emily
  Graeme 157
  Hannah 157
  James 157
  John 109
  Samuel Angus 48
Mary
  Elaine 128
Masing
  Tatiana 94
Mason
  Laim Aaron 81
  Scott 81
  Sunni Alicia 81
Masters
  Kelly 117
  Mary 35
Matheson
  Christina Anne 162
Mayne

Index

Alan Todd 73
Barry Leeland 73
Brenda Elaine 73
Carol Anne 73
James Kevin 73
Janice Catherine 73
Kenneth Trent 73
Leland Paynter 73
McColl
  James 200
McConchie
  David 84
McConnell
  Dianne 106
  Jim 106
  Kim 106
  Nancy 106
  Susan 106
McDonald
  Donald 1, 2, 8, 164, 172, 173, 174, 204
  Duncan 177
  Finlay 177
  Peter 177
  Sadie 111
McGlenn
  Joanne Acorn 79
  Willa Acorn 79
McInnis
  Grant 78
  James 78
  Janice 78
  Sarah 78
McKenna
  Nancy 95
McKinnon
  John 184
McNamara
  John 46
Mearns
  Heath Donald 65

Holt MacKenzie 65
  Jerad Wayne 65
  Wayne 65
Meery
  George 92
  Leo 92
Meier
  Andy 80
  Lance Andrew 80
  Lori-Anne 80
Melville
  P. 49
Merritt
  Mike 96
Millar
  Allan 65
Miller
  Charlotte Louise 129
  David Rike 77
  Gary 77
  Grace 157
  Jack Thomas 129
  Laura 79
  Margaret 139
  Noreen Joyce 122
  Paris Natalie 77
  Pat 85
  Rike David 77
  Stephen 129
Mitchell
  Catherine 41
  David 41
  Gordon 41
  James 41
  John 41
  Mary 41
  Michael 41
  Robert 41
  Thomas 41
Moeller
  Rolf 157

Mood
  Charles Gordon 134
  Charles Wayne 134
  Cheryl Karen 134
  David 135
  Diana Lee 135
  Donna Louise 134
  Gordon Leslie 134
  Harold Emmet 134
  Karen Gail 134
  Richard Bradley 135
  Stephen David 135
  Susan Nancy Mood
  William Robert 135
Moore
  Rosalyn 94
Morrison
  Anne Shirley 65
  Peggy Ann 98
Moug
  Linda 155
Muller
  Gerald 95
  Kristie Melissa 95
  Stephanie Leigh 95
Mullin
  Abbie 93
  Angelina 93
  John 93
  Tena 93
Munro
  Alexander 36
  Amanda 36
  Bonnie 97
  Donald 36
Murley
  Damon Chad 68
  Stephen 68
Murnaghan
  Anna 119
Murphy

Dale 36
Murray
  Heather 155
  Yvone Catherine 68
Mutch
  Alexander 43
  Cecilia 44
  Theophillius Mutch 163. See also David Theodore

N

Neal
  Joe 141
  Patrick 141
Neil
  Jack John Neil. See Donald John MacLeod
Nicholson
  David 97
  Douglas 37
  Geordie 37
  James 37
  Randolph 37
  Sarah 37, 162
Nolan
  Anna Marie 68
Norris
  Irene 142

O

Oatway
  Beverly 37
O'Dresgal
  Bonnie 122
Ogden
  Gary Lee 134
Olcott
  Harriet 132
Oldfield
  Sandra 117
Olsen
  Darren John 121
  Jakob Darren 121
  Jenna Lynn 121
  Megan May Lanette 121
Olson
  Jessica Kristen 35
  Steven 35
Oosterhuis
  Margaret Susan Leigh 99
  Marlo 99
  Regan Sara Jane 99
Orne
  Jean 40
  Jerrold 40
  Jonathan 40
  Mary 40

P

Pagani
  Louis Frank Anthony 86
Peabody
  A.P. 61
Pellett
  Tamara Bernice 121
Penner
  Cody 88
  Heidi 88
  Marvin 84
  Pamela 88
  Tricia 88
Penny
  Jackie 155
  Shirley 117
Perfect
  James Peter 121
  Kendra Lynn 121
Peters
  Dean 84
  Kimberly 68
Peterson
  Cathy 132
  Richard 132
  Robert 70
  Terry 132
Philippson
  Karla 87
Phillipo
  Carl 102
  Emily 102
  Grace 102
Phillips
  Brian 79
  Eric 79
  Jennifer 79
  Lori 79
  Michael 79
Piper
  Dorothy 142
Polapeck
  Helen 105
Pownall
  Angela 66
Preciado
  Gloria Alvira 77
Pretty
  Theresa Lynn 86
Price
  Rosie 106
Profitt
  Drew 68
  Emma 68
  Mike 68
  Nicolas 68
Pronovost
  Marcel 129
Properzi

Sharon 83
Prosser
  Lorna 70
Proud
  Lori Anne 64
Proude
  Dan Russell 68
  Gordon Russell 68
  Gregory Owen 68
  Kristen Rae 68
  Patricia Dawn 68
Provost
  George 97
  Laurie 97
  Mark 97
  Ryan 97
Pycock
  Catherine 41
  Elizabeth 42
  Jane 41
  Norman 41
Pycock-Kassar
  Julia 42
  Laura 42

R

Rafuse
  Evangeline 94
Rattray
  Margaret 39
Raymond
  Emmalee Anne Rayond 66
  Gary Edgar 66
  Graeme Edgar Douglas 66
  Kaitlyn Ruth 66
  Scott David 66
Reeves
  Marion Noreen 73
  Richard 109

Renfrew
  James 82
  James Robert 82
  Janelle 82
  Jeanne Arlene 82
  Jim 82
  Judy Lynn 82
Richmond
  Ada 80
  Richard Boston 35
  Richard 35
  Yvonne 87
Rijken
  Christian 85
  Jordon 85
  Miriam 85
  Rachel 85
  Ronald 85
Roach
  Lorraine 144
  Patrick Joseph 144
  Pat 144
Robbins
  Edith Lillian 33
  Percy 33
Roberts
  Amelia Dawne 95
  Amy Lynn 98, 123
  Brittany Skye 95
  John 98, 123
  Karen 143
  Lance 95
  Mathew 98, 123
  Timothy 98, 123
Robertson
  Alice 156
  Calum 156
  Charles 155
  Colin 156
  David 155
  Flora 156
  Hannah 156

  Madeleine 156
  Maelle 156
  Neil 156
  Noa 156
  William 156
Robinson
  Gordon Carter 116
  Guy 84
  James 115
  Kassy Marie 115
  Kyasha Arrielle 85
  Paul 81
  Veshalla 85
Rodger
  Charles Peter 80
Rogers
  Alex 38
  John Thomas 38
  Kristie 38
Roggeveen
  Charles 68
  Kees Charles 68
Rose
  Patricia 83
Ross
  Bobby 105
  Donald 31
  Erin Todd 88
  Ewen 28
  Gordon 105
  Harvey 105
  Joel Allan 116
  John 28
  Kent William 116
  Kim Murdock 88
  Lonnie Wayne 88
  Mary 31
  Reg 87
  Tracy 85
  William 116

S

Samms
  Marty 98, 123
Samuels
  Cheryl 85
Sanders
  Ron 83
Sanderson
  Angela Lynne 67
  Jody John 68
  Kathy Diane 68
  Marcia Helen 68
  Robert Carlyle 67
Sandwith
  Carly Christine 87
  Earl 86, 87
  Elizabeth Rita 86
  Emily Samantha Kate 86
  Hamish 87
  James Gerald 87
  James 87
  Joan Margaret 86
  John Robert 86
  Jordon Thomas 87
  Kenneth 86, 87
  Mary Joy 87
  Mary 87
  Michael Earl 87
  Sara Anne Marie 87
  Spencer Thomas 87
  Thomas David 87
  Tom 86
  William Ian 86
  Zoe Oliva 87
Santo
  Peter Jason 76
  Richard Allen 76
Saunders
  Ken 92
  Rebecca 92
  Scott 92
  Shawn 92
Sausa
  Arthur 75
Savage
  James 142
  Jason 142
  Jeff 142
  John 142
  Joseph 142
  Sarah 142
Sawula
  Shelly 86
Sayre
  Nancy 133
Scally
  Roco 142
Schmaus
  Don 87
Schramm
  Jean 141
Scott
  Julia 64
  Mary Ann 64
  Munroe 151
  Norman 63
  Peter 64
  Ronald 155
  W. Wilson 155
Seibert
  Kay 85
Shaver
  Terry 42
Shaw
  Ernest 137
  Isabel 107
  Katherine 137
  Sharon 78
Shearer
  Catherine 42
Shepherd
  Terry 86
Sherren
  Charles Edward 70
  Gordon Bell 70
  Hazel Mae 70
  Irene Rose 70
  James Wilfred 70
  Myron Robert 70
Silliker
  Olive MacNeill 97
Simerly
  David 133
  Dianne 133
  Eric 133
  James 133
  Kathryn 133
  Kyle 133
  Richard 133
  Sean Mac 133
Simpson
  Elaine 155
Sincennes
  Benjamin Samuel 127
  Emily Elizabeth 127
  Nicholas Alexander 127
  Pierre 127
Sinclair
  Karen 71
  Wendell 73
Sipocz
  Frank Imre 84
Skinner
  Jacob 67
  Jake 67
Slawson
  Roger 97
Smesney
  Rudy Quentin 108
  Tara Isabelle 108
Smith
  George Alexander

Index

 105
Karen 105
Shelly 63
Smyth
 Blaine 137
 Kaye 137
 Kelly Anne 137
Snider
 Charlene 88
 Jessica 88
 Kimberly 88
Spencer
 Heather Louise 87
Squarebriggs
 April 68
Stanley
 Brian Earl 72
 Carol Marie 72
Staynor
 Amanda Faye 121
 Steven 120
Stead
 Frances 97
Stephenson
 Anne-Marie 134
Stevens
 Sharon 81
Stewart
 Alyssa 137
 Anna 36
 Bonnie 36
 Braeden 137
 Butch 36
 Catherine 28, 162
 Christan 174
 Donald 161
 Emma 36
 Halle 36
 Jack 158
 Jayson 36
 Jonathon 36
 Lillian 108

 Martin 36
 Scott 36
 Sheldon 137
 Wade 36
 William Ewen 158
Stillman
 Edith 138
Stockbridge
 Charles 134
 Lindsay 134
 Rebecca 134
Stokes
 Elizabeth 33
Strickland
 Florence 163
 Sherren 163
Stymeist
 Alexander Munroe 142
 Amanda Jo 141
 Barbara Jean 141
 Betty Catherine 142
 Buddy 142
 Colleen 141
 David 141
 Denyse 141
 Edmond 140
 Edward Allen 141
 Janelle Nicolle 141
 Jessie Emiline 142
 John 141
 John Thomas 141
 John William 141
 Joseph Gerard 141
 Joseph Sanders 140
 Lou 142
 Marcia 141
 Melissa Louise 141
 Melody 141
 Robert 141
 Sandra 141

 Steven 141
 Theodore Munroe 142
 William Amos 141
 William 140
Sweet
 Debby 70
Swenson
 John 75
Swingle
 John Leonhardt 76
 Laurie Alexandra 77
 Peter Jason 77
Switzer
 Janice 80
Syll
 Janine 133
Szekely
 Margit 98, 123

T

Tackett
 Andrea Ervine 132
 James 132
 Mike 132
 Paul Ervine 132
Taggert
 James 44
 John 47
Tarras
 Andrea 128
 Gordon 128
 Jefferson 128
Taylor
 Aaron Joseph 117
 Alan Cecil 69
 Amber Ellen Irene 117
 Brian James F. 117
 Cathy Lynn 69

Cecil Perley 69
Chantelle Ellen
   Elizabeth 117
Chantelle 113
Christopher Ryan
   118
Daniel 117
David 69
Edison 113, 114,
   115, 117
Eleanor Louise 69
Elizabeth Anne 69
Elsa Merle 117
Harold Collings
   117
Hazel Adelaid 65
Heather Ruth 69
John 44, 47
Krista 69
Lillian 149
Louise Elizabeth
   117
Luke Jonathon 99
Margaret Elizabeth
   62
Margaret Leah 115
Marion 116
Matthew Taylor
Michael D.J. 117
Myrtle Alberta 67
Prudence Amelia
   133
Prudence Elizabeth
   116
Rebekah Marie
   Anne 117
Roderick 113, 117
Ronald William
   Edison 117
Rowland 99
Samantha Nicolle
   117

Samuel Judson 117
Shawn Gordon 117
Sidney 61, 62, 65,
   67, 69
Wendell Brian 117
William Edison
   117
William 61, 133,
   149
Telford
   Natasha 108
   Raymond 108
   Ryan 108
   Selby 108
   Taylor 108
Terry
   Roy 34
Tervit
   Elizabeth Ann 44
Theodore
   David 163. See
      also Theophil-
      lius Mutch
Thomas
   Cecil Henry 75
   Christina 69
   Dolina Alice 75
   Elva Wellington 75
   Ewen Earl 76
   James Alfred 61, 75
   James Samuel 75
   James 61, 69
   Jane 75, 88
   Jim 88
   Libby 61, 65, 67, 69
   Mary Elizabeth 61
   Myrtle Alexandra
      75
   Olive Maude 75
   Rebecca Margarite
      75
Thomson

Jo 156
Thurston
   Chase 96
   Irene 96
   Lila 96
   Molly 96
   Robert 96
   Rodney 96
   Trevor 96
Todd
   Annie Elizabeth 71
   Carl Robert 73
   Catherine Jane 72
   Daniel Earl 73
   David Earl 73
   Ella Mae 70
   Hazel Christena 73
   Jackie Walter 73
   James Ewen 70
   James Melvin 73
   James Robert 69
   James 74
   Jim 59
   Kelsie Murray 70
   Margaret Frances
      70
   Olive Maude 73
   Samuel Robert 69
   Thelma Elaine 74
   Vaunda Joan 70
   Violet Rebecca 73
Tollhurst
   Nancy 150
Tomison
   Anne 155
Trainor
   Barbara 69
Traver
   Barbara 77
Treget
   Eric Brent 84
   Katherine Judith 84

Robert Ewart 84
Ted 84
Trodden
  Norma 127
Tryhurn
  David Allan 80
  Kyle Cody 80
Tubert
  Shawn 136
Tuftin
  Braiden 85
  Colton Ross 85
  Darren Lowery 85
  Dean Nelson Dennis 85
  Nels 85
Turcotte
  Manon 67
Tweedie
  Bonnie Jean Frances 78
  Craig 78
  Eric Lamont 78
  Hugh John 78
  John 78
  Loran 78
  Michele Elizabeth 78
  Patrick 78

U

Underhay
  William 113
Ungar
  Michael 128
Ungar-Campbell
  Megan 128
  Scott 128
Upton
  Debby 63

V

VanIderstine
  Gladys 37
  Peter 37
Verbal
  Virginia 96
Vickers
  Margaret May 121
Villa
  Anne Marie 93
Volpe
  Alicia Victoria 35
  Anthony David 35
  Steven 35

W

Wagner
  Jennifer 132
  J.R. 132
Walanski
  Michael 136
  Trevor 136
Walker
  Andrea Shirley 66
  Andrew David 66
  Annie 74
  Brodie William 66
  David Brian 66
  David Leroy 65
  David Sidney 65
  Debra Catherine 66
  Edwin Winston 67
  Janice Adelaide 66
  Joan Deborah 66
  John 74
  Kimberly Anne 67
  Kory Justin 66
  Margaret Elizabeth 65
  Patricia Rae 66
  Peter Wayne 66
  Sarah Elizabeth 66

Sharon Lynn 67
Troy Dillion 66
Wallace
  Carol Joann 73
Walsh
  Christopher 108
  Clint 108
Ward
  Alberta Shirley 77
  Albert 76
  Frederick Warner 77
  Jennifer 36
  Lillian Frances 76
Wark
  Catlyn 63
  Jonathan 63
  Michael 63
  Michelle 63
Warren
  Charlotte 162
  Willard Webster 163
Webster
  Carla 39
  Nancy 39
Weeks
  Calvin 123
  Carson Varey 123
Weiss
  Sherry 80
Wellington
  Fred 75
Westgate
  Frances 141
Westlie
  John 8, 118
Wethington
  Linda 141
Whalen
  Edward 70
Wheatly

Arthur Blair 63
Dillon 64
Gordon Arthur 64
Marlene Lorna 63
Nancy Elizabeth 64
Sydney 64
Taylor 64
White
　Debbie 38
　John Reddie 163
Whiteway
　Edith 36
Willett
　Brendan Timothy 121
　Donald George 120
　Timothy Eifion 121
　Wendy Margaret 120
Williams
　Andrew James 129
　Benjamin Michael 128
　Carline 129
　Chris 141
　Collin 129
　Jenny 141
　Jerry 141
　John 132
　Julia Elizabeth 128
　Katherine Anne 128
　Kimberly Sandra 128
　Mark 129
　Paul 76
　Ronald Edgar 128
　Winton 128
Williamson
　Kenneth 16, 20, 21, 22, 24
Wilma

Judith 82
Wilson
　Amanda Mary 95
　Elsie Hickox 95
　Jack 75
　Jean 93
　John 75
　Steve 95
Winchester
　Lena 73, 74
Winsor
　Arnie 73
With
　Jacob Bryan 81
　Rachael Jasmine 81
　Tony 81
　Zakery Andrew 81
Wood
　Darren 117
　Elijah Roderick 117
　Gavin Robert 117
Wright
　Emily 122
　Nicholas 122
　William 122

Y

Yearout
　Lisa 80
　Robert 79
　Stephanie 79

Z

Zakem
　Paul 71
Ziegler
　Barry 92
　George 92
Zintel
　John Stephen 76

www.ingramcontent.com/pod-product-compliance
Lightning Source LLC
Chambersburg PA
CBHW072003110526
44592CB00012B/1186